the Stories of our SAVIOUR

First published in 2011 by Striving Together Publications, a ministry of Lancaster Baptist Church, Lancaster, CA 93535. Striving Together Publications is committed to providing tried, trusted, and proven books that will further equip local churches to carry out the Great Commission. Your comments and suggestions are valued.

Striving Together Publications
4020 E. Lancaster Blvd.
Lancaster, CA 93535
800.201.7748

Cover design by Andrew Jones
Layout by Beth Lee
Layout Design by Craig Parker
Edited by Danielle Mordh
Contributors:
Joanne Bass   Taniia Hymer
Terrie Chappell   Alyssa Lofgren
Tim Christoson   Lisa Harris
Billy Willis

ISBN 978-1-59894-160-9
Printed in Canada

Contents

How to Use This Curriculum

A Series of Thirteen Lessons

This curriculum series, *The Stories of Our Saviour*, focuses on thirteen parables told by our Lord Jesus Christ during His earthly ministry. These stories are presented in a unique and simple format.

The Life of Christ

This series is part of a larger, four-quarter, fifty-two lesson series on the life of Christ. The other three series include *The Signs of Our Saviour*, which focuses on our Lord's miracles; *The Steps of Our Saviour*, which focuses on the events which occurred early in Jesus' earthly ministry; and *The Sacrifice of Our Saviour*, which focuses on the betrayal, crucifixion, resurrection, and ascension of Christ.

Class Time

Each lesson contains sufficient resources to fill a ninety-minute class period. For those attempting to use the curriculum for a sixty-minute class period, we suggest the teacher choose which resources would be most effective and use them accordingly.

Age Appropriateness

This curriculum and its accompanying resources have been written for use with elementary-age children. Those who teach preschool-age children will also find it compatible for use with ages four and under.

Ideas & Resources Included

Experts suggest that we can estimate the average child's attention span as one minute per year of life. For example, those teaching eight-year-olds should expect to change activities in the classroom every eight minutes or so, in order to keep the students' attention. The one exception to this rule would be the main Bible lesson itself. During the Bible lesson, attention can be kept through the combined use of visual aids such as flash cards, objects, role-play, digital projection, and a chalk/dry-erase board.

Included in Every Lesson:

One-Page Lesson Snapshot

At the beginning of each lesson is a summary page, intended to be photocopied by the teacher and tucked into his or her Bible for ready reference. This page may also be distributed to the assistant teachers in advance, so they may prepare for their classroom responsibilities. This page includes each week's lesson title, Scripture references, memory verse, lesson outline, and a suggested class schedule.

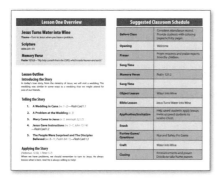

Scripture Passage

Great teaching begins with God's Word! Teachers should study the included Scripture passage numerous times throughout the week, make notes, and become familiar with the passage.

Teacher's Checklist

Use the weekly checklist to gather the appropriate materials in preparation for Sunday. Instructions may be given to an assistant teacher to pick up the needed items for the suggested craft, snack, game, or object lesson. The checklist identifies additional items found on the Ministry Resource CD (sold separately).

Snack Suggestion

Children will enjoy a different snack each week, which will not only be a treat but also a reminder of the truth learned. This is a fun and tasty way to give children a break during their time in the classroom.

Lesson Introduction

As each week's lesson begins, thought-provoking questions are asked, as students consider their own real-life circumstances, similar to those they will encounter in the Scripture. As you enter the lesson, allow for a brief period of answers and open discussion.

Verse-by-Verse Bible Lesson

Each lesson surveys a select portion of Scripture taking a walk of discovery through the biblical record. Lessons are divided into easy-to-identify points with helpful cross references included.

Lesson Application

At the conclusion of each lesson, the teacher should seek to remind students of one or two primary truths to take away from the story. Then ask, in practical terms, how children might apply those truths during the week. At this time in the lesson, students who would like to receive Christ as Saviour should be encouraged to speak to a trained counselor.

Review Game with Questions

A unique theme-oriented game is included in each lesson for the purpose of review. While other questions may be added by the teacher, a list of initial review questions designed to reinforce the lesson are provided for use during the game.

Teaching the Memory Verse

A creative way of teaching the week's memory verse is included in each lesson. The Visual Resource Packet (sold separately) includes visuals for use with each memory verse. These visuals are also available on the Ministry Resource CD (sold separately).

Object Lesson

Children will remember the five-minute object lessons designed to support the Bible lesson. Each object lesson is easy to teach and simple to prepare using objects most of us have at home or that are available at a retail store.

Craft

Each lesson includes a craft that students and parents will enjoy putting on display! The craft section includes a supply list, easy-to-follow directions, and simple thoughts on how it relates to the Bible lesson.

Teaching Tips

Creative ideas and suggestions are provided for the purpose of effectively delivering the truths contained in each week's lesson.

Teacher's Note

Historical notes, practical instructions, and biblical definitions are provided to assist the teacher in study and preparation.

Suggested Visual Aids:

The "mixing up" of the weekly visuals will keep students engaged and will prevent predictability.

Flash Cards

In the thirteen lessons, flash cards are used to illustrate the Bible story (three cards for each story). Find the icon in the lesson margin to show each flash card to the students at the appropriate time. These thirty-nine flash cards are included in the Visual Resource Packet (sold separately).

Act It Out

In certain lessons, we suggest selecting students to help "act out" the Bible story. Vary your choices in order to give all students who wish to be involved the opportunity to do so throughout the course of the series. The students more eager to participate in this role play are likely those who will benefit most from the exercise.

Draw It!

Many classrooms are equipped with a chalk or dry-erase marker board. Included in the margin of select lessons are simple sketches that even the most artistically-challenged teacher can draw! We suggest that you have the students draw along with you to reinforce the events taking place in the story.

Use an Object

Some weeks, teachers may utilize a physical object to keep students' attention. Suggested props of this nature are found at strategic points in the margin of the Bible lesson.

The Ministry Resource CD:

We recommend that each church or class purchase the Ministry Resource CD and make the files available to as many teachers as desired. This enables the investment in the CD to be spread over an unlimited volume and time.

Coloring Pages

Younger children (roughly three-year-olds through 3rd grade) will enjoy coloring a scene from each week's Bible lesson. Share an original copy with each teacher and provide as many photocopies as needed for all classes, one per student.

Activity Pages

Older children (roughly 3rd through 6th grades) will enjoy creative activities related to each week's Bible lesson. Activities include word searches, crossword puzzles, mazes, and brainteasers. Share an original copy with each teacher and provide as many photocopies as needed for all classes, one per student.

Student Take-Home Paper

The take-home paper is designed to help students take the Bible truth into the week ahead as they leave the classroom. Take-home papers will remind students of the weekly memory verse, include additional review questions, and suggest practical ways for applying the lesson in everyday experiences. Share an original copy with each teacher and provide as many photocopies as needed for all classes, one per student.

PowerPoint Presentation

A Microsoft PowerPoint presentation is available for each of the thirteen lessons. If you have a television, computer monitor, or projector available, children will enjoy being able to follow the main points of the lesson on the screen. Each week's memory verse is also included in the presentation. These presentations are fully editable, and may be shared with as many teachers as desired. Feel free to move the PowerPoint files from the CD to your own computer, and to add or edit slides as you wish.

Memory Verse Visuals

The same visuals included in the Visual Resource Packet are included in PDF form on the Ministry Resource CD. These are provided so that teachers may use the images in projection or another form, including providing copies to students.

Craft and Game Templates

Throughout the series, templates are utilized with select crafts and games. These templates are found on the Ministry Resource CD in PDF form.

Suggested Classroom Schedule

Before Class		Complete attendance record. Provide students with coloring activity pages.
Opening		Welcome
Prayer		Prayer requests and praise reports from the children
Song Time		
Memory Verse		James 1:22
Song Time		
Object Lesson		Reaping Your Seed
Bible Lesson		The Sower and the Seed
Application/Invitation		Help saved students apply lesson. Invite unsaved students to receive Christ.
Snack		Caramel Apples
Review Game/ Questions		Seed Packets
Craft		Sowing Seed
Closing		Give announcements and pray. Distribute take-home papers.

Lesson One Overview

The Sower and the Seed
Theme—Allow the seed of God's Word to grow in your heart.

Scripture
Matthew 13:3–9, 18–23

Memory Verse
James 1:22—*"But be ye doers of the word, and not hearers only, deceiving your own selves."*

Lesson Outline

Introducing the Story
In today's lesson, we will hear a story from Jesus. Imagine yourself in the crowd of people to whom Jesus is talking. Pretend that right there in front of you, Jesus is talking. Let's hear what He has to say.

Telling the Story

1. **The Farmer Sows His Seed** (v. 3)

2. **Seed Scattered Everywhere** (vv. 4–8)—*Flash Card 1.1*

3. **The Wayside Soil** (v. 4)

4. **The Stony Soil** (vv. 5–6)

5. **The Thorny Soil** (v. 7)—*Flash Card 1.2*

6. **The Good Soil** (v. 8)—*Flash Card 1.3*

Jesus Explains the Story (Psalm 81:11, 2 Timothy 2:3, 4:3a,
Hebrews 3:13, Psalm 1:1–3, Galatians 5:22–23)
Jesus tells us what each soil means and how it applies to our lives.

Applying the Story
Which soil are you? When your heart is like the good soil, you can share the

1 Lesson One

The Sower and the Seed

Theme: Allow the seed of God's Word to grow in your heart.

Scripture

Memory Verse

James 1:22
"But be ye doers of the word, and not hearers only, deceiving your own selves."

Matthew 13:3–9,18–23

3   *And he spake many things unto them in parables, saying, Behold, a sower went forth to sow;*

4   *And when he sowed, some seeds fell by the way side, and the fowls came and devoured them up:*

5   *Some fell upon stony places, where they had not much earth: and forthwith they sprung up, because they had no deepness of earth:*

6   *And when the sun was up, they were scorched; and because they had no root, they withered away.*

7   *And some fell among thorns; and the thorns sprung up, and choked them:*

8   *But other fell into good ground, and brought forth fruit, some an hundredfold, some sixtyfold, some thirtyfold.*

9   *Who hath ears to hear, let him hear.*

18   *Hear ye therefore the parable of the sower.*

19   *When any one heareth the word of the kingdom, and understandeth it not, then cometh the wicked one, and catcheth away that which was sown in his heart. This is he which received seed by the way side.*

20   *But he that received the seed into stony places, the same is he that heareth the word, and anon with joy receiveth it;*

21   *Yet hath he not root in himself, but dureth for a while: for when tribulation or persecution ariseth because of the word, by and by he is offended.*

22   *He also that received seed among the thorns is he that heareth the word; and the care of this world, and the deceitfulness of riches, choke the word, and he becometh unfruitful.*

23   *But he that received seed into the good ground is he that heareth the word, and understandeth it; which also beareth fruit, and bringeth forth, some an hundredfold, some sixty, some thirty.*

Teacher's Checklist

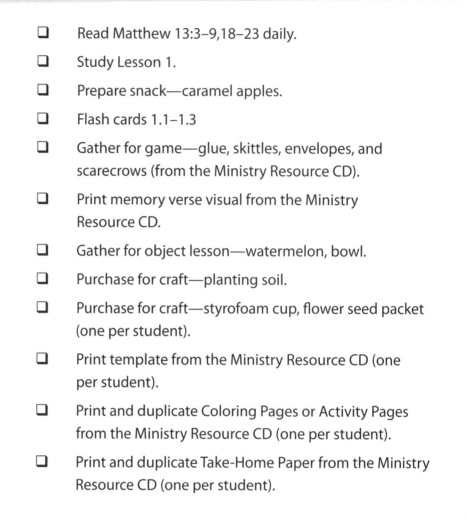

- ❏ Read Matthew 13:3–9,18–23 daily.
- ❏ Study Lesson 1.
- ❏ Prepare snack—caramel apples.
- ❏ Flash cards 1.1–1.3
- ❏ Gather for game—glue, skittles, envelopes, and scarecrows (from the Ministry Resource CD).
- ❏ Print memory verse visual from the Ministry Resource CD.
- ❏ Gather for object lesson—watermelon, bowl.
- ❏ Purchase for craft—planting soil.
- ❏ Purchase for craft—styrofoam cup, flower seed packet (one per student).
- ❏ Print template from the Ministry Resource CD (one per student).
- ❏ Print and duplicate Coloring Pages or Activity Pages from the Ministry Resource CD (one per student).
- ❏ Print and duplicate Take-Home Paper from the Ministry Resource CD (one per student).

Bible Lesson

Scripture: Matthew 13:3–9,18–23

INTRODUCING THE STORY

Have you ever been reading a story, or listening to a story, and before you knew it, you saw yourself in the story? I mean, have you ever thought what it would be like to be a particular character in the story? Have you ever felt what it would feel like to be that character? Well, when Jesus told a story, that's exactly what He wanted His listeners to do. He wanted us to think, "I wonder where I fit into this story? If I were there, which character would I be? How would I act if I were that character? How would I feel if I were that character?"

Jesus sat by the seaside, and people came just to be near Him and to hear what He would say and to see what He would do. In fact, so many people came to Jesus that He decided to get into a boat and go out from the land a little so everyone could see and hear Him. Try to see yourself in that crowd of people. Can you see in your mind's eye the enormous, clear blue sky, the fluffy clouds, and the sparkling sea that seemed to go on and on forever? And right there in front of you, is Jesus in a boat. You are surrounded by a multitude of people—people just like the ones in this room today—so many people that you weren't able to see Jesus at all until He climbed into that boat. There you all are, waiting to hear what Jesus will say and to see what Jesus will do, and He has a story just for you. As you listen to Jesus' story, see if you can determine which character you are in His parable, or story.

THE STORY

1. The Farmer Sows His Seed (v. 3)

There was once a farmer. It was planting time for this farmer, but before he could plant his seed, he needed to cultivate the ground. That means he had to dig it up and make it nice and soft and free of weeds so the seed could germinate (sprout) and grow. He dug up the soil with a pick and a hoe, carefully working his ground until the soil was prepared to receive his seed. All the while he worked, he thought of his wife and children, and he felt a

Draw It!

great sense of satisfaction as he labored to provide for their needs. The day came when the field was ready for him to take his basket of seed to sow in his field. The farmer kissed his wife and hugged his children, reminding them that he was going to plant seed in order to produce a bountiful harvest to provide for their needs all next winter and spring; and he started out toward his field.

All winter the farmer had been saving seed from last year's crop, and now the sun was shining warmly on his back. His plowed field looked so inviting, and it was a perfect day for planting. The farmer took all of this in, and he felt excited. He could hardly wait to begin sowing his seed.

Flash Card 1.1

Draw It!

2. Seed Scattered Everywhere (vv. 4–8)

When he got to his field, he happily began scattering seed. He wanted a bountiful crop, so he scattered seed all over the field. As the farmer tossed his seed, some of the seed fell onto parts of his property that weren't prepared for the seed. Some seed fell on the pathway through his huge field. Some seed fell in areas of his field that had hard stones right under the top of the soil. Some seed fell beside the field into the weeds and thorns, but some of the seed fell right where the farmer wanted it to fall—on his good ground. Jesus told us what happened to the seed that fell on all those different types of soil.

3. The Wayside Soil (v. 4)

Jesus taught first about the seed that fell by the wayside. He said, "Some seeds fell by the way side, and the fowls came and devoured them up:" (Matthew 13:4). This was the seed on the pathways. The ground was packed down hard from people walking on the paths, so it wasn't soft enough for the seed to sink into the soil. Birds flying overhead saw the seed sitting on top of the soil, and they swooped down and devoured every last seed that had fallen by the wayside. The seed provided a very easy meal for hungry birds, and it was gone before it could even begin to grow.

4. The Stony Soil (vv. 5–6)

Next, Jesus told what happened to the seed that fell on the stony places. "Some fell upon stony places, where they had not much earth: and forthwith they sprung up, because they had no deepness of earth: And when the sun was up, they were scorched; and because they had no root, they withered away" (Matthew 13:5–6). The seed that fell on the stony places had just a little soil above the stones. The seed sprouted very quickly, but their roots didn't have enough soil to develop properly and they were unable to reach down deeply into the soil to get water and minerals to strengthen and nourish the young plants. Without a strong root system, the plants that sprang up from the seed in the stony places just withered away under the scorching sun.

5. The Thorny Soil (v. 7)

Then Jesus told what happened to the seed that fell into the thorny places. "And some fell among thorns; and the thorns sprung up, and choked them:" (Matthew 13:7). The thorns grew more quickly than the plants, and the thorns took all the nourishment out of the soil so the plants from the seed couldn't get what they needed in order to survive. The strong roots of the thorns choked the smaller roots of the farmer's plants, so the farmer's plants couldn't grow. The plants that came up from the seed in the thorny places were choked to death without ever producing fruit for the farmer and his family.

Flash Card 1.2

6. The Good Soil (v. 8)

But some seed fell on the good ground which had been carefully prepared by the farmer; and Jesus said about this seed, "But other fell into good ground, and brought forth fruit, some an hundredfold, some sixtyfold, some thirtyfold" (Matthew 13:8). This seed did just what the farmer had hoped it would do. This seed was what the farmer had in mind back in the spring on that happy planting day when the sun had warmed his back so encouragingly. This seed was going to provide for the needs of his family

Flash Card 1.3

Draw It!

until next year's harvest. Yes, this seed did just what seed is supposed to do—it brought forth fruit!

Have you guessed which character you are in Jesus' story about the farmer? (This story is often called The Parable of the Sower. Allow time for discussion as to which character the children think they would be.) Your character (and mine) is actually something you wouldn't normally think of as a character at all, but Jesus had a wonderful way of using the ordinary things around us to teach us the really important lessons of life. You are the soil. Jesus is the Sower, and the seed is the Bible, God's Word.

JESUS EXPLAINS THE STORY

Jesus went on to tell us what this story meant. He said, "When any one heareth the word of the kingdom, and understandeth it not, then cometh the wicked one, and catcheth away that which was sown in his heart. This is he which received seed by the way side" (Matthew 13:19). Jesus said the hardened soil by the wayside is like a heart that is hard—one that isn't listening. It is a heart that isn't interested in God's Word. The devil (just like the birds) comes and snatches away the seed of God's Word that was sown on that hard, disinterested, disobedient heart.

> **Psalm 81:11**
>
> 11   *But my people would not hearken to my voice; and Israel would none of me.*

Next, Jesus explained the stony ground. He said, "But he that received the seed into stony places, the same is he that heareth the word, and anon with joy receiveth it; Yet hath he not root in himself, but dureth for a while: for when tribulation or persecution ariseth because of the word, by and by he is offended" (Matthew 13:20–21). The stony ground is like a heart that is very excited to hear God's Word at first (anon—at once, immediately). The person with a stony heart loves to hear about miracles and exciting things God does and says, but he doesn't let the Word of God change him. He doesn't let the Word of God sink deep down into his heart. After awhile, when problems come into the life of this person with a stony heart, he or she becomes discouraged, displeased, and offended by God's Word.

2 Timothy 2:3

3   *Thou therefore endure hardness, as a good soldier of Jesus Christ.*

2 Timothy 4:3a

3a   *For the time will come when they will not endure sound doctrine.*

Jesus went on to teach about the thorny ground. "He also that received seed among the thorns is he that heareth the word; and the care of this world, and the deceitfulness of riches, choke the word, and he becometh unfruitful" (Matthew 13:22). The thorny ground is like a heart that wants to take in God's Word, but doesn't want to allow God to clean out the sin that he or she has been allowing to grow there. Just as the thorns choked the good seed, the sin that is allowed to remain in a heart chokes the seed of the Word of God. The person with a thorny heart is deceived (tricked) into believing that money and things of this world will make him or her happy. This person might believe that if he has the latest video game, a cell phone or laptop of his own, or shoes like his friend, he would be satisfied with his life. Another might think that a new purse or outfit, a bedroom decorated like her friend's, or a new hairstyle would be the key to a happy life. If these thorns were removed from this heart, the person would be able to understand the truth that only God and His Word bring fulfillment and happiness.

Hebrews 3:13

13   *But exhort one another daily, while it is called To day; lest any of you be hardened through the deceitfulness of sin.*

Finally, there was the good ground. Jesus said, "But he that received seed into the good ground is he that heareth the word, and understandeth it; which also beareth fruit, and bringeth forth, some an hundredfold, some sixty, some thirty" (Matthew 13:23). Jesus said that when seed is sown into good ground, it brings forth fruit. A heart that is like the good ground is one that is soft and able to take in the seed of God's Word and allow it to grow. When the seed of the Word of God grows in a heart, it produces fruit that can be seen in a person's life.

Psalm 1:1–3

1   *Blessed is the man that walketh not in the counsel of the ungodly, nor standeth in the way of sinners, nor sitteth in the seat of the scornful.*

2   *But his delight is in the law of the LORD; and in his law doth he meditate day and night.*

3   *And he shall be like a tree planted by the rivers of water, that bringeth forth his fruit in his season; his leaf also shall not wither; and whatsoever he doeth shall prosper.*

Some of the fruit in a "good-ground" heart are found in Galatians, and we call them the "fruit of the Spirit," because they are produced in our lives through the Holy Spirit.

Galatians 5:22–23

22   *But the fruit of the Spirit is love, joy, peace, longsuffering, gentleness, goodness, faith,*

23   *Meekness, temperance: against such there is no law.*

Yet another fruit that grows in a "good-ground" heart is the desire to plant the seed of the Word of God in other hearts, sharing the truth of God's Word and salvation with others.

APPLYING THE STORY

So, which kind of soil is your heart?

Wayside soil

When a preacher or teacher shares God's Word, are you interested, or

- Do you allow your mind to wander and think of other things?
- Do you whisper with your friends?
- Do you pass notes? (Teacher, add whatever behavioral issues you detect in your students during class.)

If you do these things, you are letting the truth of God's Word slip away, just like the seed that fell by the wayside.

Stony soil

Are you excited about what you hear in a sermon or Sunday school lesson, but then you don't allow God's Word to really change your life?

- If the message is about honoring your parents, do you happily obey your parents when you get home? Or do you talk back when they ask you to clean your room?

- If the sermon is about reading your Bible and praying, do you choose a specific time to spend with the Lord every day? Or do you just think, "I do need to read my Bible and pray," but you never set aside a time to do it, and then it doesn't happen?

- If the lesson is about honesty, do you tell the truth about a lie you have told and ask forgiveness for lying? Or do you just try to hide from your guilty feelings until they go away?

- When the sermon is about soulwinning, (sharing the Gospel with others) and you know the Holy Spirit is telling you to share the Gospel with someone, do you share it as soon as possible? Or do you put it off until later, and then you don't feel the desire to share it anymore?

When hard times come do you become discouraged and offended? Do you stop doing the right things that God has already taught you when you go through difficult times? If so, you are allowing your heart to be like the stony soil where the seed sprouts quickly, but soon dries up.

Thorny soil

Are you like the thorny soil? Do you like what you hear from God's Word, but you just don't want to let go of the sin and love for other things that you have allowed in your heart?

- Do you spend so much time getting ready for school or church in the morning that you don't have time to read the Bible and pray?

- Are you unkind to someone at school so you can be accepted by a classmate, even though you know God's Word tells you to be kind to everyone?

- Do you spend your money on things you want, but you don't give money in the offering at church, even though you know God wants you to tithe (give 1/10 of your money to Him) and give to missionaries?

Teaching Tip

When discussing trials that can cause your students to be discouraged, you could list specific hard circumstances that apply to your individual students. For example: divorce of parents, loss of a parent's job, bully at school, death of a grandparent or sibling, etc. These could, and should, include more common situations, as well, such as: sibling rivalry, a friend or sibling having broken their favorite toy or game, being denied a privilege or possession they wanted, etc.

- Do you follow your friends in doing wrong, even though you know God's Word says, "My son, if sinners entice thee, consent thou not." (Proverbs 1:10)?

Good soil

Or, when you hear or read God's Word, do you listen, ask God to apply it to your life, happily obey it, and then share it with others? If so, your heart is like the good soil that brings forth good fruit—just as the farmer plans for it to do.

Jesus is a perfect farmer. When soil is brought to Him, He can perfectly clean out the thorns; He can move the rocks; and He can break up the hard parts. If the soil of your heart hasn't been good soil, you can ask Jesus right now to clean and change the soil of your heart to make it good soil that will not only hear God's Word, but will allow God's Word to grow in it.

I am going to pray, and as I pray, if the Lord has spoken to you about some soil that needs to be softened in your heart, right now, quietly in your heart, ask God to forgive you and to make the soil of your heart good. (Pray.)

When your heart is the good soil, you can have the joy of being two characters in Jesus' parable. Not only are you the good soil, but you can also become the sower. You become a sower when you share the seed of God's Word with others. You can bring forth fruit.

Seed Packets

Materials Needed

- Glue
- Skittles
- Envelopes
- Scarecrows from the Ministry Resource CD

Set Up

Purple = 10,000 points
Yellow = 5,000 points
Red = 3,000 points
Green = 2,000 points
Orange = 1,000 points

Print out the scarecrows and cut into fourths. Glue each scarecrow onto an envelope. Put a few skittles in each "seed packet" (they should all be different).

Divide the class into teams. After answering a review question correctly, students may choose an envelope. Open and calculate points (see chart above). Award points to the team, and the students can enjoy the candy.

1. What is a parable?
   Answer: A story

2. Who told this parable or story?
   Answer: Jesus

3. This story had three main components. Each item represented something very important. Who does the Sower represent?
   Answer: Jesus

4. What does the seed represent?
   Answer: The Bible

5. What does the soil represent?
   Answer: Us/our hearts

6. There are four different types of soil mentioned in our story. What are they?
    Answer: Wayside soil, stony soil, thorny soil, good soil

7. Each soil had unique characteristics that affected the growth of the seed. What type of soil (or heart) should we want to cultivate?
    Answer: Good soil

8. What kind of heart does the wayside soil represent?
    Answer: A hardened heart

9. What are some ways we can become discouraged, and as a result, hinder the growth of God's Word in our hearts?
    Answer: Answers will vary based on examples given during the lesson

10. When we allow God's Word to grow in our hearts, what type of fruit will we bear with our lives?
    Answer: The fruit of the Spirit (Galatians 2:22–23) and the fruit of seeing other people come to know Jesus

Teaching the Memory Verse

James 1:22

22   But be ye doers of the word, and not hearers only, deceiving your own selves.

Print the memory verse from the Ministry Resource CD onto colored cardstock.

Play a quick game of Simon Says. Have all the students stand. Give out commands—some without saying "Simon Says." If the students do the command without hearing "Simon Says" then they have to sit down. Also, if a student does not do the command when hearing "Simon Says" he will have to sit down. (Have other workers help determine who is out.) The last one standing wins.

The only way to win at this game is to hear the command and then obey it. Life is not a game, but if we want to "win" or succeed in our Bible reading we must not only hear God speaking to us, but understand what He says and do that which He commands.

After playing Simon Says, have students open their Bibles to James 1:22. Read the verse several times, then pass out each of the flash cards to select students. On the count of three, have the students, without talking, arrange themselves in correct verse order. If the students do not complete correctly, begin again—this time allowing them to talk it out. Repeat this exercise until each student has had a turn (or until time runs out).

Object Lesson—Reaping Your Seed

Objects needed:

You will need to have a small watermelon (not a seedless watermelon) cut up into several pieces. There should be one small piece of watermelon for each child. As they eat the watermelon have them place all the watermelon seeds into a single bowl. Have them guess how many seeds may be in the bowl. The teacher should count the seeds and then say, "Isn't it amazing that by planting just one watermelon seed, we get this delicious watermelon and all these additional watermelon seeds? If we planted all these seeds we would have more watermelons than we would know what to do with!"

One plant can bring forth many plants because of all the seeds it possesses. When we allow the seed of the Word of God to grow in our hearts, great things will come out of our lives. We will be kind, we will reach other people with the Word of God, and the fruit of the Spirit will grow in our lives. When we do reach someone else with the Word of God, the seeds will begin to grow in their heart, and they will then be able to lead someone to Christ.

Additional Resources

Find the following items on the Ministry Resource CD:

- Coloring Page (for younger children)
- Activity Page (for older children)
- Student Take-Home Paper
- PowerPoint Presentation

Craft—Sowing Seed

Getting It Together

Materials needed:
Yellow construction paper
Seed
Planting soil
Crayons
Glue
Scissors

Per student:
1 styrofoam cup
1 boy craft template located on the Ministry Resource CD
1 heart verse template located on the Ministry Resource CD
1 flower seed packet

Putting It Together

1. Print and cut out 1 heart verse and boy craft template for each student. You may print it in black and white and have the students color it, or you may print it in color.
2. Cut out yellow or tan construction paper to go around the styrofoam cup. You may have the children decorate the cup also.
3. Glue the heart verse template to the front of the cup.
4. Glue the boy template to the back of the cup.
5. Plant seeds in the cup.

Seeing It Together

The seed planted in the good soil can help us remember that Jesus wants our hearts to be like the good soil. This planting cup can remind us to tell everyone about Jesus' love.

Suggested Classroom Schedule

Before Class		Complete attendance record. Provide students with coloring/activity pages.
Opening		Welcome
Prayer		Prayer requests and praise reports from the children
Song Time		
Memory Verse		Ephesians 4:32
Song Time		
Object Lesson		Forgive!
Bible Lesson		The Unforgiving Servant
Application/Invitation		Help saved students apply lesson. Invite unsaved students to receive Christ.
Snack		Royal Scepters
Review Game/ Questions		Speed Ball
Craft		Door Hanger
Closing		Give announcements and pray. Distribute take-home papers.

Lesson Two Overview

The Unforgiving Servant

Theme—Be quick to forgive.

Scripture
Matthew 18:21–35

Memory Verse
Ephesians 4:32— *"And be ye kind one to another, tenderhearted, forgiving one another, even as God for Christ's sake hath forgiven you."*

Lesson Outline
Introducing the Story
Today we will meet a man who chose to believe what Jesus told him. He chose to believe the promise that Jesus made, and he was not disappointed!

Telling the Story
1. **The King and His Servants** (v. 23)

2. **The King Collects Debts Owed Him** (vv. 23–24)

3. **The Servant's Plea for Mercy** (vv. 25–26)—*Flash Card 2.1*

4. **The King's Compassion** (v. 27, Lamentations 3:22)

5. **The Servant's Unforgiveness** (vv. 28–30)—*Flash Card 2.2*

6. **The Servant Punished** (vv. 29–34, James 2:13)
   —*Flash Card 2.3*

Applying the Story *(Philippians 2:13, Luke 6:36, Ephesians 4:32)*
God is the Great Forgiver. When we have been forgiven of our sins against God, we have a choice to forgive others' sins against us. Every time someone sins against you, remember how good God is to you.

2 Lesson Two

The Unforgiving Servant

Theme: Be quick to forgive.

Scripture

Matthew 18:21–35

21 Then came Peter to him, and said, Lord, how oft shall my brother sin against me, and I forgive him? till seven times?

22 Jesus saith unto him, I say not unto thee, Until seven times: but, Until seventy times seven.

23 Therefore is the kingdom of heaven likened unto a certain king, which would take account of his servants.

24 And when he had begun to reckon, one was brought unto him, which owed him ten thousand talents.

25 But forasmuch as he had not to pay, his lord commanded him to be sold, and his wife, and children, and all that he had, and payment to be made.

26 The servant therefore fell down, and worshipped him, saying, Lord, have patience with me, and I will pay thee all.

27 Then the lord of that servant was moved with compassion, and loosed him, and forgave him the debt.

28 But the same servant went out, and found one of his fellowservants, which owed him an hundred pence: and he laid hands on him, and took him by the throat, saying, Pay me that thou owest.

29 And his fellowservant fell down at his feet, and besought him, saying, Have patience with me, and I will pay thee all.

30 And he would not: but went and cast him into prison, till he should pay the debt.

31 So when his fellowservants saw what was done, they were very sorry, and came and told unto their lord all that was done.

32 Then his lord, after that he had called him, said unto him, O thou wicked servant, I forgave thee all that debt, because thou desiredst me:

33 Shouldest not thou also have had compassion on thy fellowservant, even as I had pity on thee?

34   *And his lord was wroth, and delivered him to the tormentors, till he should pay all that was due unto him.*

35   *So likewise shall my heavenly Father do also unto you, if ye from your hearts forgive not every one his brother their trespasses.*

Teacher's Checklist

- ❑ Read Matthew 18:21–35 daily.
- ❑ Study Lesson 2.
- ❑ Flash cards 2.1–2.3
- ❑ Gather props for lesson—robe and crown for king, play money for taxes, signs for servants.
- ❑ Prepare snack—fruit, cheese, plastic skewer.
- ❑ Gather for game—nerf ball, treats.
- ❑ Print memory verse visual from the Ministry Resource CD.
- ❑ Gather material for object lesson—pencils with erasers worn off.
- ❑ Purchase for craft—foam craft letters, decorative accents, foam craft door hanger, glitter glue.
- ❑ Print and duplicate verse template for craft.
- ❑ Print and duplicate Coloring Pages or Activity Pages on the Ministry Resource CD (one per student).
- ❑ Print and duplicate Take-Home Paper on the Ministry Resource CD (one per student).

Royal Scepters
Fruit and cheese kabob scepters—layer strawberries, grapes, melons, and cheese on a plastic skewer.

Bible Lesson

Scripture: Matthew 18:21–35

INTRODUCING THE STORY

Jesus often talked to His followers (called disciples) about ordinary situations. He wanted them to know God's directions to people in order for them to live their everyday lives in the way God had planned. Just as your dads and moms give you instructions to teach you how to live, God gave instructions to show us how to live as Christians.

One of the most important lessons Jesus taught His disciples was to forgive others. As Jesus spoke to them about forgiveness, Peter came to Him with a question: "Lord, you have told us to forgive. If someone sins against me over and over again, how many times should I forgive him? Should I forgive him seven times?"

Jesus gave Peter an amazing answer. He looked into Peter's eyes and said, "I say not unto thee, Until seven times: but, Until seventy times seven" (Matthew 18:22).

Peter must have thought, "Whoa! I thought I was doing good in thinking I would forgive someone seven times! Now Jesus is telling me to forgive them so many times I wouldn't even be able to keep track of all those times!" That gave Peter the understanding that Jesus meant Peter shouldn't count how many times someone sinned against him. He should just forgive and forgive and forgive and keep on forgiving—over and over. Peter knew it would be hard to be so forgiving.

Jesus knew He needed to explain with a story.

THE STORY

1. The King and His Servants (v. 23)

There was once a king who had many servants. Some of the servants were the king's hunters. They went out hunting every morning so the king could have fresh meat on his table every evening. Some of his servants were chefs and bakers. They prepared scrumptious, delicious, kingly meals to set before the king and his court. Some of his servants cleaned the castle, and some sewed royal clothing for the king and his family. Some of the servants fed, trained, and groomed the king's beautiful horses.

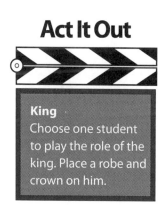

Act It Out

King
Choose one student to play the role of the king. Place a robe and crown on him.

The king also had other servants who went throughout the kingdom collecting taxes from the people. The king would tell the tax-collector servants how much money each person owed in taxes. (Now, the king allowed these servants to charge the taxpayers extra money, so the servants would have some money to keep for themselves. That was how these servants made a living for their families.) Then, the tax-collector servant would go to each person who owed taxes to the king and say, "The king has ordered your taxes to be paid today." The servant would tell the person the amount he owed, including the amount for the servant to keep for himself. The person who owed the money would pay the servant, and the servant would pay the king, keeping the extra for himself.

2. The King Collects Debts Owed Him (vv. 23–24)

It was time for the king to call in all the servants who owed money to the king.

One after another, the king's servants stood before him to pay the money they owed. Some owed the king for land they rented from the king, and they would pay the rent. Some owed the king for money they had borrowed from the king, and they would pay off the loan. Some owed the king for the taxes they had collected, and they paid the taxes.

There was one servant in particular who came before the king. In fact, Jesus said that this servant was *brought* before the king. It seems this servant didn't even want to come to the king on his own, but he had to be brought.

This particular servant owed the king so much money that he would never be able to pay it. The amount this servant owed the king was, in those days, called "ten thousand talents." In our day, this amount would be millions and millions of dollars!

This servant was not rich. He wasn't a millionaire or a billionaire—he was just a servant of the king. Perhaps he had been a tax-collector servant and had spent all the tax money he had collected, rather than giving the king what he owed him. Whatever his job was, he now owed the king more money than he could ever earn in his whole lifetime—and the king was telling him to pay it all right now!

Act It Out

3. The Servant's Plea for Mercy (vv. 25–26)

Well, the servant couldn't pay the debt, and the king made a decision that greatly frightened the servant. The king said, "I command that this servant be sold. Not only shall this servant be sold, but his wife shall be sold, as well. Not only shall this servant and his wife be sold, but his children shall be sold. They all shall be sold as slaves, and everything they own shall be sold. After the servant, his wife, his children, and their belongings are all sold, the money is to be brought to me in payment for this servant's debt."

The servant was horrified. He fell down at the king's feet. He cried to the king, "Lord, have patience with me, and I will pay thee all." He was so afraid of losing all that he had that he didn't even think about the fact that he really could never pay the king all that money. All he could think about was losing his wife, his children, and his belongings, and being sold as a slave. He just couldn't let that happen, so he begged the king to give him a chance to pay the debt.

Flash Card 2.1

Act It Out

Servant
The servant gets on knees and begs the king. The king compassionately forgives the servant and lets him and his family go free.

4. The King's Compassion (v. 27)

The good king looked at the servant who was crying at his feet. The king thought about how he would feel if he were in his servant's place. He thought what it would be like to lose everything he had and to be sold as a slave. The king thought about his own children and how he would never want them to be sold.

As the king looked at the servant and thought about the hardship the servant's family was about to face, the king's heart filled with compassion. "Then the lord of that servant was moved with compassion, and loosed him, and forgave him the debt" (Matthew 18:27). The king said, "Servant, arise. I forgive you of your debt. Not only am I not going to sell you, your wife, your children, and all that you have, but I will not make you pay me even one penny that you owe me. Your debt is wiped away—you are forgiven of your debt!"

Teacher's Note

Mercy:
"the disposition that tempers justice and induces an injured person to forgive trespasses and injuries, and to forbear punishment, or inflict less than law or justice will warrant"

Lamentations 3:22

22   *It is of the LORD'S mercies that we are not consumed,*
     because his compassions fail not.

Can you imagine the joy of the servant? He had owed the king more money than he could ever pay, and now he owed absolutely nothing! He had been brought before the king owing a great debt, and now he left the king's presence free, owing nothing.

Act It Out

Servant
The servant holds a sign that reads 100 pence. Act out the servant requesting the man for payment.

Act It Out

Fellow Servant
He begs for mercy. The servant who was just forgiven does not forgive and casts him into prison.

Flash Card 2.2

5. The Servant's Unforgiveness (vv. 28–30)

The servant's joy didn't last long. He soon forgot how good the king had been to him. He forgot about the great amount of money he had owed the king. He forgot how merciful the king had been to him in not selling him, his wife, their children, and all their belongings. He forgot how relieved he was in being forgiven of his great debt.

The servant's mind wandered to another man—a fellow servant of the king's—who owed this first servant a little money. This fellow servant owed him what was called in that day an hundred pence. In our day, the amount would be about fifteen dollars.

As the servant thought about his fellow servant who owed him fifteen dollars, anger began filling his heart. Angry thoughts began going through his mind. "He owes me money, and he is making no effort to pay me! I need money to feed my family. I need money to pay my taxes. Who does he think he is, not paying his debts? I need that money he owes me." The servant began looking for the fellow servant who owed him fifteen dollars.

At last he found his fellow servant, and by now he was so angry that he couldn't speak kindly to him. He grabbed his fellow servant by the throat and shouted, "Pay me that thou owest," (Matthew 18:28). "Give me my money this instant."

The poor fellow servant—he didn't expect this man to come to him today! The fellow servant fell down at the first servant's feet, just as the first servant had fallen down before the king. "Have patience with me, and I will pay thee all," (Matthew 18:29) the fellow servant pleaded, just as the first servant had pleaded with the king. But, the first servant was not patient or forgiving, and he had his fellow servant thrown into prison!

6. The Servant Punished (vv. 29–34)

Other servants of the king were watching everything. They had seen the king command that the first servant be sold. They had heard that it was not only the servant who would be sold, but his wife, their children, and all they owned. They had watched the first servant fall down before the king, begging the king to be patient with him. They had been glad as the king said, "I forgive you of the debt—you owe me nothing."

But the servants had also seen the first servant go to his fellow servant. They saw him grab his fellow servant by the throat. They had heard him tell his fellow servant to pay him all he owed. They had watched as the fellow servant fell down before the first servant, pleading with him to be patient with him. They had been saddened as they saw the servant cast his fellow servant into prison, telling him he must remain there until he had paid every cent he owed the first servant.

These servants who had watched everything went to the king. They told the king what they had seen. They described how the servant who had been forgiven a great debt by the king did not forgive his fellow servant a small debt, but had cast him into prison.

The king called for the servant whose debt he had forgiven. "I forgave you that great debt because you pleaded with me to do so," the king said to his servant. "But you—you didn't forgive your fellow servant who owed you a very small amount of money! Don't you think you should have had compassion on your fellow servant, as I had compassion on you?"

The king became very angry with his servant. "You will be thrown into prison," he said, "until you pay me every cent you owe."

Flash Card 2.3

James 2:13

13 *For he shall have judgment without mercy, that hath shewed no mercy; and mercy rejoiceth against judgment.*

APPLYING THE STORY

This story is often called "The Parable of the Unforgiving Servant," and Jesus told Peter and the other disciples what He wanted them to learn from it. He told them the story was to teach them to forgive from their hearts (Matthew 18:35). He wanted the disciples to learn to forgive from way deep down in their hearts—not just from their minds.

Do you know the difference between forgiving from your mind and forgiving from your heart? When you forgive from your mind, you still have angry feelings in your heart, even after you say, "I forgive you," or "That's okay." It may be that your brother broke something that was special to you, and you were angry at him. Then, when your mom saw or heard what was going on, she said to you, "Now, Tyler, you need to forgive your brother." So, you said, "I forgive you." But you still felt that anger toward him in your heart. That is forgiving from your mind.

Another time, maybe your sister borrowed a book from you, and she left it out and the dog chewed on it. Now your book was ruined! You might have

Teaching Tip

Your students each have their own set of circumstances for which they need to learn to forgive from their hearts. Some are universal, as many listed here. Some are unique to a particular student, and you can include some of those unique circumstances in this list as you teach. Alternately, you can talk individually with a student who is suffering from the effects of an unforgiving heart.

said, "Hailey, why did I let you borrow my book? You never put stuff away, and now the dog ruined my book!" Then, you looked at Hailey, and you thought about how you really do love her. You thought about how sometimes you don't put things away, and the dog could chew on them just as easily as he had chewed on your book. You thought about how awful it must seem to Hailey to have you acting so angry toward her. You felt sorry inside, and you realized that anyone could have done what she did. You told her you forgave her, and you meant it from your heart. That is forgiving from your heart.

Every day of your life things will happen to you for which you need to forgive someone from your heart.

- Your sister wears your outfit without asking your permission.
- One of your parents punishes you for something you didn't do.
- Your brother loses your baseball glove.
- Your friend breaks a game you loaned her.
- Someone at school calls you a name.
- Someone lies about you.
- Your best friend leaves you for another best friend.
- Your mom or dad leaves your home.
- Your dad gets drunk and doesn't keep a job.
- Your teacher corrects you in front of the whole class, and you don't feel you deserve it.
- Your sister or brother messes up your room.

The disciples knew it would be hard to forgive over and over again. In fact, when Jesus told Peter that we are to forgive as many times as someone sins against us, the disciples said to Jesus, "Lord, Increase our faith" (Luke 17:5). We can't always forgive from our heart if we try to do it by our own power. It takes faith in God to really forgive from our hearts, and He promises to help us if we ask Him.

Philippians 2:13

13   *For it is God which worketh in you both to will and to do of his good pleasure.*

God is the Great Forgiver. In fact, God is like the king in Jesus' parable of the unforgiving servant. We are the servants. We owe God a very great debt—so great that we could never pay it. That debt is our sins. There is nothing we can do to pay for our sins, but Jesus paid the entire debt for our sins when

He shed His blood for us on the Cross. When we ask Jesus to forgive our sins, and we trust Him as our Saviour, God forgives the whole debt we owe Him. We can be very joyful that God frees us from our sin and forgives our debt through Jesus.

When we have been forgiven of our sins against God, we have a choice as to whether we will forgive others' sins against us. Every time someone sins against us, we can remember how good God is to us. We can think of the great debt we owed God. We can think of how every sin we have ever committed was against Him. We can think of how He loved us so much that He sent His Son to die in our place so we wouldn't have to pay for our own sins in the Lake of Fire. We can think of how we are free and forgiven, even though we don't deserve it.

Then, we can look at the person who has wronged us. We can think of how small their sin against us is compared to our sin against God. We can think of how Jesus suffered for our wrong. We can think of how much God loves them—just like He loves us! We can ask God to increase our faith and make us more like Jesus, helping us to forgive. Forgiveness is part of God's plan to give us joyful lives and to make us more like Jesus.

Luke 6:36

6   *Be ye therefore merciful, as your Father also is merciful.*

Maybe you have never asked Jesus to be your Saviour from sin, and you don't know the joy of having your sins forgiven. When you trust Jesus as your Saviour, and God forgives your sin debt, you will find God's forgiveness is even better than when the king forgave the debt of millions of dollars the servant owed him. When you ask Jesus to forgive your sin and be your Saviour, you will be able to spend all eternity in Heaven with Jesus.

If Jesus is your Saviour, He wants to help you forgive others, just as He forgave you. Think about your life this week. Think about who wronged you. Do you still feel anger or bitterness in your heart toward those who wronged you? Right now, in your heart, you can ask God to fill you with the same forgiveness He gave you. You can ask Him to help you forgive each person who wronged you for each time they wronged you. He will help you forgive from your heart.

Ephesians 4:32

32   *And be ye kind one to another, tenderhearted, forgiving*
        one another, even as God for Christ's sake hath forgiven you.

Review Game/Questions

Speed Ball

Materials Needed

- Small nerf ball
- Treats

Instructions

Have students quickly toss the nerf ball to any other student. When the teacher says "STOP," whoever is left holding the ball answers the question. If the student answers correctly, give him/her a little treat.

1. What question did Peter ask Jesus that prompted Jesus to tell the story?
   Answer: How many times should I forgive?

2. What did the king's servants help the king do?
   Answer: Collect money (taxes)

3. What did the king command to be done to the servant who could not pay his debts?
   Answer: He commanded that he be sold into slavery (along with his family).

4. What did the servant do when he heard he was to be sold into slavery?
   Answer: He begged for mercy.

5. When the servant asked for mercy, did the king become angry or was he moved with compassion?
   Answer: He was moved with compassion.

6. How did the king demonstrate his compassion and mercy?
   Answer: He forgave the large debt of the servant.

7. Did the forgiven servant forgive others?
   Answer: No!

8. Who does the king represent, and who do the servants represent, in our story?
   Answer: The king represents God, and the servants represent us.

9. What is the greatest debt that has ever been forgiven and paid?
    Answer: Jesus paid for our sin debt on the Cross.

10. Name some ways you can express forgiveness to others.
    Answer: Answers will vary but may include examples given on page 34.

 Teaching the Memory Verse

Ephesians 4:32

*32   And be ye kind one to another, tenderhearted, forgiving one
another, even as God for Christ's sake hath forgiven you.*

Print memory verse from the Ministry Resource CD.

We cannot control the way others treat us, but we can control the way we respond to them. It isn't always easy, but with the Lord's example and His help, we can respond correctly by loving and forgiving!

Have students open their Bibles to Ephesians 4:32. Read the verse together, then hand out each of the flash cards to students who will hold them before the class. Have the class say the verse together a few more times, then remove one flash card and have the class recite the verse. Continue removing flash cards and reciting the verse until there are no more flash cards.

Object Lesson—Forgive!

Objects needed:

A large assortment of pencils with worn or no erasers

Scripture:

Matthew 18:21–22

21 Then came Peter to him, and said, Lord, how oft shall my brother sin against me, and I forgive him? till seven times?

22 Jesus saith unto him, I say not unto thee, Until seven times: but, Until seventy times seven.

What to say:

Just look at all of these pencils! There are short pencils, long pencils, skinny pencils, and fat pencils. There are yellow, red, black, and white pencils. There are many different shapes, sizes, and colors of pencils—but there is one thing that all of these pencils have in common: the eraser is worn off of every one of them. Do you know what that tells me? It tells me that I make a lot of mistakes! When I make a mistake, I erase it and start over again, until I get it right! I don't know why I keep these pencils, because with all the mistakes I make, a pencil without an eraser is pretty useless.

These pencils remind me of people. People come in all different sizes, shapes, and colors, but we all have one thing in common: we all make mistakes! We make a lot of mistakes. But when we do something wrong, we can ask God to forgive us; and because of Jesus, He will forgive our mistakes and we can start over again and again and again. Unlike these pencils, God's eraser never wears out!

Just as God forgives us over and over again. Jesus taught us that we should forgive other people over and over again.

One day, Peter asked Jesus, "How many times should I forgive someone who sins against me? Should I forgive him seven times?" I imagine that Peter was pretty proud of himself for being willing to forgive someone seven times.

Jesus answered, "Not seven times, but seventy times seven times!"

I think Jesus knew that if He said we should forgive seventy times seven times, we would never be able to keep count, and we would forgive over and over again, just as He forgives us. It doesn't matter if we are short or tall, red, white, yellow, or black, we all need God's forgiveness.

Craft—Door Hanger

Getting It Together

Glitter glue
Foam craft letters and decorative accents

Per student:
Foam craft door hanger
Lesson 2 craft verse template

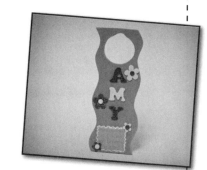

Putting It Together

1. Print and cut out Lesson 2 craft verse template.
2. Have the children decorate the foam craft door hanger.
3. Glue the verse to the bottom of the foam craft hanger by outlining it with the glitter glue.

Seeing It Together

This door hanger can help you remember that Jesus commanded us to forgive others no matter what they have done.

Additional Resources

Find the following items on the Ministry Resource CD:

- Coloring Page (for younger children)
- Activity Page (for older children)
- Student Take-Home Paper
- PowerPoint Presentation

Suggested Classroom Schedule

Before Class	Complete attendance record. Provide students with coloring/activity pages.
Opening	Welcome
Prayer	Prayer requests and praise reports from the children
Song Time	
Memory Verse	Deuteronomy 6:5
Song Time	
Object Lesson	Have Compassion
Bible Lesson	The Good Samaritan
Application/Invitation	Help saved students apply lesson. Invite unsaved students to receive Christ.
Snack	Hershey Hugs
Review Game/ Questions	L-O-V-E
Craft	Kindness Coupons
Closing	Give announcements and pray. Distribute take-home papers.

Lesson Three Overview

The Good Samaritan
Theme—Love and help others like Christ loves and helps us.

Scripture
Luke 10:25-37

Memory Verse
Deuteronomy 6:5—"And thou shalt love the LORD thy God with all thine heart, and with all thy soul, and with all thy might."

Lesson Outline
Introducing the Story (Psalm 147:5, 19:19b, Deut. 6:5)
The story we will look at today is the parable of the Good Samaritan. We will learn what it truly means to love someone.

Telling the Story
1. **A Man Takes a Journey** (v. 30)
2. **The Traveler Is Beaten and Robbed** (v. 30)—*Flash Card 3.1*
3. **A Priest Happens By** (v. 31)
4. **A Levite Happens By** (v. 32, 1 John 3:17–18)—*Flash Card 3.2*
5. **A Samaritan Happens Along** (v. 33a)
6. **The Samaritan Shows Compassion** (vv. 33b–35)
   —*Flash Card 3.3*

Applying the Story (Galatians 6:2)
Just as the Good Samaritan in the story showed compassion to someone who was a stranger to him, you can show compassion to the people in your life. God wants to make you a good neighbor—a Good Samaritan.

3 Lesson Three

The Good Samaritan

Theme: Love and help others like Christ loves and helps us.

Scripture

Memory Verse

Deuteronomy 6:5
"And thou shalt love the LORD thy God with all thine heart, and with all thy soul, and with all thy might."

Luke 10:25–37

25 And, behold, a certain lawyer stood up, and tempted him, saying, Master, what shall I do to inherit eternal life?

26 He said unto him, What is written in the law? how readest thou?

27 And he answering said, Thou shalt love the Lord thy God with all thy heart, and with all thy soul, and with all thy strength, and with all thy mind; and thy neighbour as thyself.

28 And he said unto him, Thou hast answered right: this do, and thou shalt live.

29 But he, willing to justify himself, said unto Jesus, And who is my neighbour?

30 And Jesus answering said, A certain man went down from Jerusalem to Jericho, and fell among thieves, which stripped him of his raiment, and wounded him, and departed, leaving him half dead.

31 And by chance there came down a certain priest that way: and when he saw him, he passed by on the other side.

32 And likewise a Levite, when he was at the place, came and looked on him, and passed by on the other side.

33 But a certain Samaritan, as he journeyed, came where he was: and when he saw him, he had compassion on him,

34 And went to him, and bound up his wounds, pouring in oil and wine, and set him on his own beast, and brought him to an inn, and took care of him.

35 And on the morrow when he departed, he took out two pence, and gave them to the host, and said unto him, Take care of him; and whatsoever thou spendest more, when I come again, I will repay thee.

36 Which now of these three, thinkest thou, was neighbour unto him that fell among the thieves?

37 *And he said, He that shewed mercy on him. Then said Jesus unto him, Go, and do thou likewise.*

Teacher's Checklist

- ❏ Read Luke 10:25–37 daily.
- ❏ Study Lesson 3.
- ❏ Flash cards 3.1–3.3
- ❏ Gather props for lesson—map of Israel, antibiotic cream, gauze, glove, pen.
- ❏ Prepare snack—Hershey hugs and kisses.
- ❏ Print and cut game pieces for review game from the Ministry Resource CD.
- ❏ Print memory verse flash cards from the Ministry Resource CD.
- ❏ Gather materials for object lesson—Band-Aids, dollar, brown bag.
- ❏ Purchase for craft—key chain ring for each student.
- ❏ Gather other materials for craft—hole punch, cardstock.
- ❏ Print the card template for craft from the Ministry Resource CD.
- ❏ Print and duplicate Coloring Pages or Activity Pages on the Ministry Resource CD (one per student).
- ❏ Print and duplicate Take-Home Paper on the Ministry Resource CD (one per student).

Snack Suggestion

Hershey Hugs
Give each child a small handful of Hershey hugs and kisses. As the children enjoy the snack remind them to show kindness and compassion on others just like the Good Samaritan.

Bible Lesson

Scripture: Luke 10:25–37

INTRODUCING THE STORY

Do you ever have questions? I hope so! One of the best ways to learn is by asking questions. I hope you have many questions and that you always take your questions to people who can answer the question correctly.

When you have a question about life, where do you think you should go to find the answer? Since God is the Creator of all life, He has the answer to every question about life. The place to go to find the correct answers to questions about life is God's Word. You can find answers in God's Word for yourself, and you can find answers by asking people who love God and study His Word.

Psalm 147:5

5   *Great is our Lord, and of great power: his understanding*
    is infinite.

Jesus has the right answer for every question. When Jesus lived on earth, people often went to Him with questions. Sometimes they really wanted to know the answer, and sometimes they just wanted to see if Jesus would make a mistake in His answer. But Jesus never made a mistake, and He never will make a mistake. He never was wrong, and He never will be wrong. No one could ever ask Jesus a question to which He didn't know the right answer.

One day a lawyer was listening to Jesus speak. The lawyer stood up and asked Jesus a question: "Master, what shall I do to inherit eternal life?" (Luke 10:25). Jesus answered by directing the lawyer to the Bible for his answer. Jesus said, "What is written in the law? how readest thou?" (Luke 10:26). Jesus knew the Bible is always right and always true.

Psalm 19:9b

9b   *The judgments of the LORD are true and*
    righteous altogether.

Teaching Tip

Display a map of Israel at the time of Christ. Point out the cities of Jerusalem and Jericho. Discuss that, though Jericho is north of Jerusalem, Jesus said the man went "down" from Jerusalem. This is because Jerusalem is situated on a hill, and every destination was "down" the hill.

The lawyer gave Jesus an answer from the Bible. "And he answering said, Thou shalt love the Lord thy God with all thy heart, and with all thy soul, and with all thy strength, and with all thy mind; and thy neighbour as thyself" (Luke 10:27).

Deuteronomy 6:5

5   *And thou shalt love the LORD thy God with all thine heart,*
    and with all thy soul, and with all thy might.

Jesus said, "You're right—do all you have just said, and you will have eternal life."

Well, the lawyer got nervous. He realized he didn't always love everyone as himself. He did love his friends, and he did love most of his family. He did love people who loved him, and he did love people who treated him kindly. But he felt a little uncomfortable about Jesus telling him he actually had to love his neighbor just as much as he loved himself. He hoped his neighbor was someone he liked.

The lawyer asked Jesus one more question, and he hoped he would like the answer. "And who is my neighbour?" the lawyer asked Jesus (Luke 10:29).

Jesus answered with a story.

THE STORY

1. A Man Takes a Journey (v. 30)

A certain man rose up very early one morning. He had a long journey ahead of him. He ate breakfast, kissed his wife, hugged his children, picked up his walking stick, and started on his way.

The business this man had to attend to must have been very important, for he was going to travel a very dangerous road—alone! For nineteen miles, from his city of Jerusalem to the city of Jericho, he would be all by himself, walking a road that everybody knew was a hiding place for thieves and robbers. All along this lonely road were huge rocks behind which thieves would keep out of sight until a lone traveler would happen by. Then, the thieves would jump out, beat up the traveler, steal his money, and run away.

2. The Traveler Is Beaten and Robbed (v. 30)

That is exactly what happened to this very traveler. He was walking along the road from Jerusalem to Jericho, when from behind a boulder (huge rock), some thieves jumped out and grabbed him. These thieves cared about no one but themselves, and their goal was to take all the money this man had. They punched and hit the man over and over. They may have stabbed the man. They kicked the man and, finally, they threw him on the ground. Not only did they steal all his money, but they stole his nice clothes as well, and they left him there alone, to die.

There the man lay on the road between Jerusalem and Jericho, not even able to stand up. He was wounded and bleeding. There was nothing he could do for himself. He lay there, alone and half dead.

3. A Priest Happens By (v. 31)

Then, a very exciting event happened. Down the road came a priest, a very religious man. Surely this priest, who taught people about God, would stop and help the wounded traveler. This priest knew all about God and God's goodness. This priest had even memorized much of the Bible by heart. Surely, this priest would want to show God's love to this wounded traveler. What a wonderful change of events for the injured man—help had arrived!

Well, things didn't go quite as well for the injured man as it seemed they would. When the priest saw the man, he did something totally unexpected. He crossed the road and walked by on the other side! He didn't walk over to the man to see exactly what was wrong. He didn't put the man on his donkey and take him to a doctor. He didn't put his jacket on him to cover his body. He didn't even call out, "I'm going to get help for you." He simply "passed by on the other side" (Luke 10:31).

4. A Levite Happens By (v. 32)

Down the road came someone else—another religious man. This man was a Levite, whose job was to work in the temple of the Lord. This Levite spent his life learning about God and serving God. This Levite would certainly stop and help the poor traveler.

Well, not only did the Levite see the wounded traveler, but he walked right up to him in order to get a better look at him. He saw the man's wounds. He saw that the man's clothes had been taken from him. He saw the man lying there, alone and half dead. He saw there was no one else to help this man.

But this Levite, whose job, remember, was to work in the temple of the Lord, also walked to the other side of the road to pass. That was exactly what the priest had done a short while earlier!

What would keep the priest and the Levite from taking care of this poor, helpless traveler? I'm sure they had excuses in their minds. Maybe they thought:

Teaching Tip

Expand the list of excuses by asking your students what excuses they think the priest and the Levite may have given.

- "I don't have time to help this man."
- "I don't even know this man—why should I help him?"
- "What if I hurt him when I pick him up?"
- "Someone might come and rob me while I'm helping him."
- "I have an appointment, and I'll be late."

Whatever excuses they made up in their minds, they didn't help the wounded man. They "passed by on the other side" (Luke 10:31b, 32b).

> **1 John 3:17–18**
>
> 17 *But whoso hath this world's good, and seeth his brother have need, and shutteth up his bowels of compassion from him, how dwelleth the love of God in him?*
>
> 18 *My little children, let us not love in word, neither in tongue; but in deed and in truth.*

5. A Samaritan Happens Along (v. 33a)

Finally, another man journeyed on the road between Jerusalem and Jericho. This man was not a religious man, as the other two had been. This man was not of the same nationality or the same religion as the injured man. This man was a Samaritan, and the injured man was a Jew. The Jews hated the Samaritans, and they would travel long distances out of their way so they wouldn't have to pass through an area where Samaritans lived. The Jews wouldn't help a Samaritan if he were in trouble or in need. The Jews didn't want to talk to a Samaritan or shake hands with a Samaritan. The Jews treated the Samaritans as if they were a lower class of people than the Jews. So, the Samaritans responded by hating the Jews, just as the Jews hated them.

This third man who came upon the injured Jew was a Samaritan, and he had very good reason to pass by on the other side—to not stop and help this wounded Jewish man. The Samaritan knew a Jewish man would never help him if he were in trouble.

6. The Samaritan Shows Compassion (vv. 33b–35)

But even so, the Samaritan did something very peculiar. He walked right over to the wounded Jew, looked at him, and "when he saw him, he had compassion on him" (Luke 10:33b). The Samaritan cared about the Jew. His heart hurt for the Jew just as if the Jew had been his own child.

The Samaritan knelt down by the injured Jewish man. He gently looked at each painful wound, and he felt extremely sorry for the man. The Samaritan reached into the traveling bag he carried on the back of his donkey, and he pulled out some medicine, oil, and cloth. He carefully, tenderly, poured medicine into each wound to cleanse it. Then, he poured oil into the wounds to help them close up and heal. Finally, he tenderly wrapped the wounds in cloth to keep them from getting dirt in them.

The Good Samaritan—which is what we call him today—didn't stop there. He didn't just look at the injured Jew. He didn't just feel sorry for him. He didn't just kneel down by him and cleanse his wounds, pouring oil on them and wrapping them in clean cloths. And he didn't pass by on the other side.

What the Good Samaritan did next was amazing. He carefully, gently lifted the wounded Jew onto his own donkey. The Good Samaritan didn't even think about the Jews and Samaritans hating each other. He didn't think about this injured man being of another nationality and another religion from his own. He only thought of the injured man's wounds, the injured man's pain, and the injured man's needs. Then, leading his donkey, with the wounded Jew lying over its back, he traveled the distance to the nearest inn, or motel.

When they arrived at the inn, the tired and kind Good Samaritan paid the innkeeper for a room. He lifted the injured man off his donkey and carried him into the inn. The Jew was suffering so badly that he didn't even realize where he was or what was happening. The Good Samaritan carried

Teacher's Note

Compassion:
"a suffering with another; painful sympathy; a sensation of sorrow excited by the distress or misfortunes of another; pity"

Teaching Tip

Bring antibiotic cream and gauze to class. As you describe the Samaritan's care for the wounded man, hold these items and pretend as if you were really dressing a wound.

Flash Card 3.3

Use an Object

A Glove and a Pen
Demonstrate how a glove cannot pick up a pen by itself. It has a shape of a hand, but it has not accomplished anything. We must invite His Holy Spirit to fill us so we can be useful to Him. Remind students how the Good Samaritan allowed the Holy Spirit to fill him and use him to serve others.

the Jew into the room of the inn and laid him on the clean, soft bed. He washed the injured man and cleansed his wounds again. He poured more oil onto the wounds and wrapped them in fresh bandages. He wrapped the man in his own clean robe. Then, the Good Samaritan lay down and drifted off to sleep.

The Good Samaritan needed to leave early the next morning. Before he left the inn, he again reached into his traveling bag, this time pulling out money. He spoke quietly with the innkeeper. "This man," the Good Samaritan told the innkeeper, "is injured very badly—he was half dead when I came upon him on the road. He was robbed and beaten by thieves. I don't know who he is, and I don't know his family. But I do know he can't take care of himself—he needs our help."

"He will need to rest in your quiet, peaceful inn. Please, take this money— it is enough to last for several days. Take care of this man. Continue nursing his wounds and cleansing him. Give him good, healthy food. He will also need clean clothes. Use the money to provide for all his needs. If you spend more money than I have given you, I will repay you when I return to your inn. Please, sir, take good care of him." And the Good Samaritan went on his way.

APPLYING THE STORY

The lawyer didn't want to hear what Jesus said next. The lawyer may have wished he had never gone to Jesus with his question, as Jesus gave him an instruction that he knew would be very hard to follow. Jesus looked kindly into the lawyer's eyes as He said, "Go and do thou likewise" (Luke 10:37).

"Go and do thou likewise" is for all of us in this room today. It means, "Do just what the Good Samaritan did." What did the Good Samaritan do that Jesus told us to do "likewise"?

- The Good Samaritan stopped to see a stranger's need.
- The Good Samaritan helped someone who he knew would probably not have helped him if he had been the one in need.
- The Good Samaritan had compassion on the stranger.
- The Good Samaritan used his own supplies to care for the stranger's injuries.
- The Good Samaritan put the stranger on his own donkey while the Good Samaritan walked.

- The Good Samaritan spent his own money at the inn to meet the stranger's needs.

The Good Samaritan, when it was time for him to leave the inn, made sure the stranger would be cared for until he was healed enough to leave.

Jesus told this story to teach us to be good neighbors, or "Good Samaritans." What would your day be like if you asked God to make you a Good Samaritan at home? At church? At school? On the playground? On the bus?

- What would you do when you have finished eating dinner and you notice your mother cleaning off the table and washing the dishes, alone?
- What would you do when your little sister needs someone to button her sweater or tie her shoe?
- What would you do when you come home from school and your little brother wants someone to play ball with him?
- What would you do when a visitor comes to Sunday school? Would you sit with him (her) and make him (her) feel welcome?
- What would you do when you see someone you don't know very well fall down on the playground?
- What would you do when you want to sit with your friends on the bus, but you notice someone sitting alone and looking lonely?
- What would you do when you are one of the captains choosing teams for a game of dodgeball or kickball? Which people would you choose? Would you choose people who aren't necessarily the best players, or would you leave them for last, hoping they are on the other team?
- What would you do if you saw someone sitting alone on the playground, crying?
- What would you do if you hear of a classmate's grandmother dying and this classmate is not your close friend?
- What would you do in the situations above if the person were a different nationality or different color than you? Would you treat them the same as you would if they were your nationality or color?
- What would you do in the situations above if the person in need had treated you unkindly in the past?

Teaching Tip

Allow time for the students to answer as you ask for ideas to encourage them to be "Good Samaritans."

Galatians 6:2

2   *Bear ye one another's burdens, and so fulfil the law of Christ.*

Just as the Good Samaritan in the story showed compassion to someone who was a stranger to him, you can show compassion to the people in your life. The Lord wants to help you show compassion to those at home, at school, at church, at the store—wherever you go. And, just as the Good Samaritan had to give up some of his own comforts, you will have to make the decision to give up some comforts of your own in order to help others. God wants to make you a good neighbor—a Good Samaritan.

Teacher's Note

You could easily end the lesson here. But if you have children in your class who are not saved, this lesson presents a great opportunity to share the Gospel.

SALVATION APPLICATION

Do you remember the very first question the lawyer asked Jesus, even before he asked, "And who is my neighbour?" The first question the lawyer asked Jesus was, "Master, what shall I do to inherit eternal life?" (Luke 10:25). The lawyer wanted to know what Jesus said about how to go to Heaven.

Jesus asked the lawyer what the Bible said about how to have eternal life, and the lawyer answered, "Thou shalt love the Lord thy God with all thy heart, and with all thy soul, and with all thy strength, and with all thy mind; and thy neighbour as thyself" (Luke 10:27).

Jesus told the lawyer that his answer was correct. But God has also told us many times throughout the Bible that no one always loves God with all his (her) heart, and no one always loves his (her) neighbor as himself (herself). Then how can we have eternal life if Jesus said we have to love God with all our hearts and love our neighbors as ourselves in order to have eternal life?

God knew that we could never love God with all our hearts and that we could never love our neighbors as ourselves at all times. So God provided a way for us to have eternal life—to go to Heaven when we die. God sent us His own Son, Jesus Christ, who always loved God with all His heart, and who did always love His neighbor as Himself. Jesus never sinned. God sent His perfect, sinless Son, to pay for our sins so we wouldn't have to pay for them forever in the Lake of Fire. He wanted us to have eternal life with Him in Heaven forever.

We are like the wounded man in the story of the Good Samaritan. We were helpless in our sins. We couldn't get up on our own. We couldn't get to Heaven on our own, because our sin kept us from God. We needed help.

We couldn't get our help from other people—people like the priest and the Levite in the story. Other people have their own sins to take care of, and there is nothing they can do about our sins.

We needed someone to have compassion on us. We needed someone to come along and cleanse us from our sins and pick us up and heal us. We needed someone to pay for our sins so we wouldn't have to pay for them ourselves.

Jesus was that Someone. Jesus had compassion on us—He knew we were dead in our sins. Jesus shed His blood on the Cross to cleanse our sins. Jesus paid for our sins with His own blood—and, just like the wounded man in the story, it didn't cost us anything! Jesus rose again from the dead so we could have eternal life with Him in Heaven forever.

Romans 6:23a

*23a For the wages of sin is **death**....* (emphasis added)

Romans 5:8

*8   But God commendeth his love toward us, in that, while we were yet sinners, Christ **died** for us.* (emphasis added)

If you have never asked Jesus to be your Saviour—if you have never asked Him to cleanse you of your sin, you can ask Him today. I will be here after class to show you from the Bible how you can have eternal life.

L-O-V-E

Materials Needed

Game pieces from the Ministry Resource CD

Instructions

Print and cut game pieces. Laminate for durability. Place game pieces in a bag. Divide the class into two teams: Blue and Green. The object of this game is to spell the word "LOVE" in their team color before the other team. Ask Team Blue a question. If the answer is correct, the student will draw a card from the bag. If the card is anything other than a "X", place that card on the matching team color. If Team Blue picks a green letter they give that card to Team Green.

1. Who asked Jesus a question before the telling of the story?
   Answer: A lawyer

2. What happened to the man in our story as he travelled from Jerusalem to Jericho?
   Answer: He was beaten and robbed.

3. Who was the first person to pass by the wounded man?
   Answer: A priest, who taught people about God, walked by.

4. What did the priest do when he the saw the wounded traveler on the side of the road?
   Answer: He passed by on the other side.

5. Who was the second man to walk past the wounded man?
   Answer: A Levite, who worked in the temple of the Lord, walked by.

6. What did the Levite do when he saw the wounded traveler on the side of the road?
   Answer: He came and looked at him, but then passed by on the other side.

7. Who was the third person to walk by the man on the road?
   Answer: A Samaritan

8. Did the Jews love or hate the Samaritans?
   Answer: The Jews hated the Samaritans.

9. How did the Samaritan show compassion toward this wounded man?
    Answer: He went to him, nursed his wounds, put him on his donkey, brought him to an inn, and paid for his needs.

10. How can we show compassion toward our neighbors (the people all around us)?
    Answer: Answers will vary.

 # Teaching the Memory Verse

Deuteronomy 6:5

5   *And thou shalt love the LORD thy God with all thine heart, and with all thy soul, and with all thy might.*

Introduce one flash card at a time. Each flash card will have a motion that goes along with the flash card. Have the class repeat it several times, then ask a student to hold that card. Show card number 2. Have the class repeat several times and then have them repeat flash card 1 and flash card 2. Continue in the same manner with the rest of the flash cards.

Motions
"And thou shalt love the LORD thy God" = Cross arms over chest.
"with all thine heart" = Trace heart shape over their heart using both hands.
"and with all thy soul" = Point to bottom of foot.
"and with all thy might" = Lift arm to side and make fist showing muscle.

Object Lesson—**Have Compassion**

Materials needed:

- Band-Aids
- A dollar
- Brown bag

Lesson Outline:

1. I have a brown bag with me today (show the brown bag). I have some things in the bag. (Pull out a couple of Band-Aids and hold them up for people to see—maybe pass them around.) Some questions you might ask:
   - Do you know what these are?
   - Have you ever had one put on you?
   - Why did you need a Band-Aid?
   - How did you feel when someone put the Band-Aid on you?

2. Show the children a dollar.
   - Do you know what this is?
   - How can you use a dollar?

3. How would you feel if while playing at a friend's house you cut yourself and started to cry? What if your friend's parents ignored you or if they said, "Hey, your pants are torn! Now you will be in trouble"? Would you say that your friend's parents were being kind?

4. Now, what would it be like if your friend's parents had given you a hug, washed the cut and then put a Band-Aid on it? (Hold up a Band-Aid.) How would you feel if they gave you a dollar to buy a popsicle? (Hold up a dollar.) Would you say that your friend's parents were kind? We should also try to be compassionate like this toward others.

Craft—Kindness Coupons

Getting It Together

Hole punch
Cardstock

Per student:
1 set of kindness cards from the Ministry
Resource CD
1 key chain ring

Putting It Together

1. Print and cut out the kindness cards on cardstock (1 set per student).
2. Punch a hole in the corner of the cards.
3. Attach the cards with a key chain ring (the kind that pulls apart).
4. On each card, instruct the students to write one kind thing they can do for others.

Seeing It Together

Jesus wants us to be kind every day. We can use these cards as a tool to remind us of ways to be kind to other people.

 # Additional Resources

Find the following items on the Ministry Resource CD:

- Coloring Page (for younger children)
- Activity Page (for older children)
- Student Take-Home Paper
- PowerPoint Presentation

Suggested Classroom Schedule

Before Class	Complete attendance record. Provide students with coloring/activity pages.
Opening	Welcome
Prayer	Prayer requests and praise reports from the children
Song Time	
Memory Verses	Psalm 55:17
Song Time	
Object Lesson	Sound Asleep
Bible Lesson	The Friend in Need
Application/Invitation	Help saved students apply lesson. Invite unsaved students to receive Christ.
Snack	Goldfish Crackers
Review Game/Questions	Big Card—Question and Score
Craft	Verse Frame
Closing	Give announcements and pray. Distribute take home-papers.

Lesson Four Overview

The Friend in Need
Theme—Be a faithful prayer warrior.

Scripture
Luke 11:5–13

Memory Verse
Psalm 55:17 — "Evening, and morning, and at noon, will I pray, and cry aloud: and he shall hear my voice."

Lesson Outline
Introducing the Story
Today's story is about a man's bedtime and how that man felt when someone awakened him from his sleep—at midnight! The man at his door desperately needed a friend.

Telling the Story
1. **A Midnight Request** (vv. 5–6)—*Flash Card 4.1*
2. **A Friend Who Didn't Want to Help** (v. 7)
3. **A Determined Friend in Need** (v. 8)—*Flash Card 4.2*
4. **The Answer to the Friend in Need** (v. 9, *James 1:17*)—*Flash Card 4.3*

Jesus Explains the Story (*Matthew 7:11*)
God is like that loving father who would not give his son a stone when he asks him for bread.

Applying the Story (*Matthew 6:33*)
Jesus told us the story of the friend in need to teach us to ask God over and over to meet our own needs. Are you asking God to help you?

4 Lesson Four

The Friend in Need

Theme: Be a faithful prayer warrior.

 ## Scripture

Memory Verse

Psalm 55:17
"Evening, and morning, and at noon, will I pray, and cry aloud: and he shall hear my voice."

Luke 11:5–13

5 And he said unto them, Which of you shall have a friend, and shall go unto him at midnight, and say unto him, Friend, lend me three loaves;

6 For a friend of mine in his journey is come to me, and I have nothing to set before him?

7 And he from within shall answer and say, Trouble me not: the door is now shut, and my children are with me in bed; I cannot rise and give thee.

8 I say unto you, Though he will not rise and give him, because he is his friend, yet because of his importunity he will rise and give him as many as he needeth.

9 And I say unto you, Ask, and it shall be given you; seek, and ye shall find; knock, and it shall be opened unto you.

10 For every one that asketh receiveth; and he that seeketh findeth; and to him that knocketh it shall be opened.

11 If a son shall ask bread of any of you that is a father, will he give him a stone? or if he ask a fish, will he for a fish give him a serpent?

12 Or if he shall ask an egg, will he offer him a scorpion?

13 If ye then, being evil, know how to give good gifts unto your children: how much more shall your heavenly Father give the Holy Spirit to them that ask him?

Teacher's Checklist

- ❑ Read Luke 11:5–13 daily.
- ❑ Study Lesson 4.
- ❑ Flash cards 4.1–4.3
- ❑ Prepare snack—goldfish crackers.
- ❑ Print Big Cards from the Ministry Resource CD for review game.
- ❑ Gather for object lesson—sleeping bag or blankets, large clock.
- ❑ Print memory verse strips from the Ministry Resource CD.
- ❑ Purchase for craft—craft sticks (4 per student), magnets (2 per student), foam stickers.
- ❑ Gather glue for craft.
- ❑ Print verse template for the craft from the Ministry Resource CD.
- ❑ Print and duplicate Coloring Pages or Activity Pages on the Ministry Resource CD (one per student).
- ❑ Print and duplicate Take-Home Paper on the Ministry Resource CD (one per student).

Snack Suggestion

To demonstrate God's goodness, give each child goldfish crackers.

Explain: If a son asked his dad for a fish, would the dad give him a snake? No! Why? Because the dad loves his son! In the same way, our Heavenly Father wants to give us good gifts.

As the children eat the crackers remind them how good God is to us. As a loving Father, He will provide for us as we ask Him.

Bible Lesson

Scripture: Luke 11:5–13

INTRODUCING THE STORY

Do you have a regular bedtime—a time when you almost always go to bed? What time is your bedtime? Have you ever been really tired at bedtime? Have you ever been so tired you could hardly think? Have you ever been so tired you maybe felt a little irritable or grouchy? Have you ever been so tired all you could think about was turning out the light and climbing into your soft, warm bed?

Jesus told a story about a man's bedtime, and how that man felt when someone awakened him from his sleep—at midnight!

The Lord Jesus had just finished praying when one of his disciples said to Him, "Lord, teach us to pray" (Luke 11:1). As Jesus taught them how to pray, He told them to ask God daily (every day) for the things they needed. He told them they should go to God over and over, day after day, asking God to meet their needs. Then, Jesus told the disciples a story to show them how important it is to pray—a story about a man's sleep being interrupted at midnight.

> **Psalm 55:17**
>
> *17   Evening, and morning, and at noon, will I pray, and cry aloud: and he shall hear my voice*

THE STORY

1. A Midnight Request (vv. 5–6)

There was a man who had a bedtime. This man's children had a bedtime. This man's wife had a bedtime. It was very important that this family had a bedtime, because they began their day early in the morning, as soon as the sun came up. At night, they would be very, very tired.

The man worked all day in his fields—planting, weeding, hoeing, and harvesting. He fed the cows, the sheep, and the donkeys. He repaired his tools. He sheared the sheep so his wife could spin the wool into thread to make clothes that would keep the family warm in the winter. He trimmed the grapevines so they would produce a large harvest of grapes. He took his sons with him into the field, and he taught them how to work with him. He worked from early morning until dark. He was very tired at bedtime.

The man's wife worked all day as well. Early each morning she prepared breakfast for her family. She packed a lunch for her husband and sons to take with them to the field. She cleaned the house, worked in the garden, and sewed clothes for her family. She held the baby on her lap as she taught her children how to read and to do their school lessons. She instructed them on how to do their chores. She made meals and clothing for her neighbors who didn't have as much money as her family had. She worked very hard, and she was very tired at bedtime.

The man's children also worked hard. They got up early in the morning and went to the well to carry buckets of water back to the house. They helped their father in the field and their mother in the house. The older children read to the younger children and helped them learn their lessons. They helped in the garden, studied their lessons, and had some time for play. The children were very tired at bedtime.

Flash Card 4.1

When bedtime came for this family, they all happily got into bed. Each one of them was so tired—even the baby went to sleep right away. Time went by as the family slept, and finally it was midnight. Everything was quiet, everything was peaceful, everyone was sleeping—when, suddenly, there was a loud knock on the door! Who could be knocking on the door at this time of night? Who would knock at midnight?

A friend of the family called through the door, "Friend, lend me three loaves; For a friend of mine in his journey is come to me, and I have nothing to set before him" (Luke 11:5b–6). The man who was knocking at the door had a friend who had come from far away to visit him. The man who was knocking at the door had no food to share with his hungry friend. The man who was knocking at the door was asking the man in bed to give him some bread so he could share it with his visitor. We will call this friend who was knocking at the door "the friend in need."

2. A Friend Who Didn't Want to Help (v. 7)

The man in the house called back through the door. He said, "Don't bother me! Can't you see the door is shut? Don't you realize my children are in bed? Don't you understand we're tired, it's midnight, and I don't want to open the door?!"

The Stories of Our Saviour | © 2011 Striving Together Publications

3. A Determined Friend in Need (v. 8)

The friend in need didn't go away. He continued to knock and kept asking for bread. The friend in need decided, "I am not going to stop knocking and I am not going to stop asking for bread until this man answers his door. I am not going to go away until he gives me some bread for my visitor."

Flash Card 4.2

The man in the house finally got up out of bed. He finally went to his pantry (food cupboard) and took out three loaves of bread. He finally carried the bread to the door, opened the door, and handed the bread to his friend in need.

The man didn't get out of bed, go to his pantry, take out three loaves of bread, open the door, and hand the bread to the friend in need because he was his friend. It was because the friend in need refused to give up. The friend in need kept knocking, asking, knocking, asking, knocking, and asking some more. The friend in need didn't give up.

4. The Answer to the Friend in Need (v. 9)

The friend in need knew the secret to getting his request answered: Keep on asking. Keep on seeking. Keep on knocking. If you ask, it will be given to you. If you seek, you will find. If you knock, it will be opened. "And I say unto you, Ask, and it shall be given you; seek, and ye shall find; knock, and it shall be opened unto you. For every one that asketh receiveth; and he that seeketh findeth; and to him that knocketh it shall be opened" (Luke 11:9–10).

The friend in need also knew that you will get exactly what you ask for. He knew that if a son asks his father for bread, the father will give him bread. A loving father wouldn't say, "Here's a stone," when his son asked him for bread—he would give him bread. If a son asks his father for a fish, the father will give him a fish. A loving father wouldn't say, "Here's a snake," when his son asked him for a fish—he would give him a fish. If a son asks his father for an egg, his father will give him an egg. A loving father wouldn't toss his son a poisonous scorpion when his son asked him for an egg—he would give him an egg. The friend in need knew that his friend would give him what he asked for, just as the father would give the child what he asked for.

James 1:17

17 *Every good gift and every perfect gift is from above, and cometh down from the Father of lights, with whom is no variableness, neither shadow of turning.*

Flash Card 4.3

With all this in mind, the friend in need kept knocking and kept asking, and finally his friend opened the door and gave him his request. The friend in need returned home in the dark of the night and shared the bread with his tired, hungry visitor.

JESUS EXPLAINS THE STORY

Jesus was explaining to His disciples that God is like that loving father, who would not give his son a stone when he asks him for bread. God is like that loving father, who will not give his son a snake when he asks him for a fish. God is like that loving father, who will not give his son a scorpion when he asks him for an egg. In fact, God is much more generous than that loving father. God is our Heavenly Father, and He wants us to come to Him, asking Him to meet all our needs.

Matthew 7:11

11 *If ye then, being evil, know how to give good gifts unto your children, how much more shall your Father which is in heaven give good things to them that ask him?*

The friend in need wasn't asking for help for himself. The friend in need wanted to help his friend who had traveled far to visit him. The friend in need didn't have anything to give his friend, so he went for help. The friend in need knew the man in the house would have bread to give to his visitor, so he went to the man in the house for help. The friend in need knew just where to go and just what to do when his friend had a need.

APPLYING THE STORY

Do you know where to go for help when your friend has a need? Who can help your friend? Your friend may have a need for which you can go to an adult to ask for help.

- Your friend may need help understanding his schoolwork. Maybe you are the one to explain it to him, or maybe you know someone else who can.
- Your friend may need her bike tire repaired. You can go to someone who has a repair kit or an air pump to find help for her.
- Your friend may have forgotten his lunch. You can share yours and ask others to share an apple or a bag of chips.
- Your friend may have a need that no one else can meet.
- Your friend's parents may be going through a divorce.
- Your friend's dad may have lost his job.
- Your friend's dog may have been hit by a car.
- Your friend may have moved away and is very lonely.
- Your friend may feel rejected by kids at school.
- Your friend may not know the Lord Jesus as her Saviour.

What do you do when your friend has a need no person can meet? Jesus told the story of the friend in need in order to teach us to pray for the needs of our friends. He told the story of the friend in need so we would ask God to meet the needs of our friends.

You can be like the friend in need, finding help from God for your friends. You can go to God over and over, day after day—asking, seeking, and knocking for the needs of your friend. God said He gives good things to them that ask Him, and you can ask God for those good things for your friend.

Then, also, you have needs. Jesus told the story of the friend in need to teach us to ask God over and over, day after day, to meet our own needs. You will sometimes have a broken heart. You will sometimes have questions for which you don't know the answers. You will have problems with your brother or sister or friend at school. Your parents may be having trouble or going through a divorce. Your parents, brothers, sisters, or other family members might not be Christians. Your parents may yell at you and treat you harshly.

As you go to God over and over, day after day, asking Him to take care of you and meet your needs, He will answer you. The friend in need received the bread he needed because he kept knocking and asking. God will meet your needs when you keep knocking and asking.

And, like the father who wouldn't give his son a poisonous scorpion, God will not give you anything that would hurt you. God will give you good things.

Act It Out

God Supplies
Choose two students. One student asks for bread. The other student gives him a stone. The student asks for a fish. The other student gives him a snake. Explain how this is not how our Heavenly Father responds to our needs. We need to ask God in prayer and He will supply. The student asks for bread. The student is given bread. (Use a delicious roll or donut.)

God wants you to keep knocking and asking so He can spend time with you. When you go to God over and over, day after day, asking Him to meet your needs, He enjoys spending that time with you. He loves you and wants you to know what a loving Father He is. He wants you to know that He is the first one you should go to when you have a need. And He doesn't want you to ever give up!

Matthew 6:33

33   *But seek ye first the kingdom of God, and his righteousness; and all these things shall be added unto you.*

Big Card—Question and Score

Materials Needed

Print "Big Cards" from the Ministry Resource CD

Instructions

Place cards face down on a table or chalkboard tray. Place all Question Cards in one stack and all Score Cards in another stack. Divide the class into teams. Have a student pick a Question Card and read the question to his team mates. Then, allow the student to call on another student from his team to answer the question. If that student answers correctly, he may pick the Score Card. Follow the instructions for awarding points. (Note: This game could have a negative total.)

Object

The team with the highest score is declared the winner.

1. What did one of the disciples ask Jesus to teach them?
    Answer: He asked Jesus to teach them to pray.

2. What time did the friend in need knock on his friend's door?
    Answer: Midnight

3. Why did the friend in need knock on the door?
    Answer: He needed bread for a visitor who had traveled a long way to his house.

4. Did the man inside the house want to help his friend?
    Answer: No, he didn't want to help.

5. Did the man in the house eventually give the friend in need some bread?
    Answer: Yes

6. Why did the man in the house give his friend the bread?
    Answer: Because the friend in need kept asking.

7. Would a loving father give a snake to his son if the son asked for a fish?
    Answer: No!

8. When we have a friend in need, to whom should we go?
    Answer: Our Heavenly Father

9. What kind of gifts does our Heavenly Father give us?
    Answer: Good gifts

10. Name some good gifts God has given you.
    Answer: Answers will vary.

Teaching the Memory Verse

Psalm 55:17

17   *Evening, and morning, and at noon, will I pray, and cry aloud: and he shall hear my voice.*

Have students turn to Psalm 55:17.

God loves to hear from us. We can talk to Him all day long and He never will tell us to stop. And, He hears us whether we shout, whisper, or silently pray. We talk to a living God who will hear and answer. The answer might not be "yes." It might be "no" or "wait." But let's remember to talk to God morning, noon, and night!

Print the memory verse strips on colored cardstock. Cut and laminate for durability. Have students take turns putting the memory verse in correct order. Record each child's time to assemble the verse. See who is the fastest at putting the verse in proper order.

Repeat the activity to reinforce the verse.

Object Lesson—Sound Asleep

Materials:
- Sleeping Bag or Blankets
- Clock

Lesson:
Choose a child to pretend that they are asleep in the sleeping bag, and set the clock to midnight. Ask the children if they have ever stayed up until midnight.

What are some things that happen at night? (Owls hoot, dogs bark, wind blows, etc.) What if someone came knocking on your door at midnight? Would you be afraid? Who would answer the door? Would you mind being awakened by a friend in need? Jesus wants each of us to know that He is never bothered when we come to Him with a need. He desires for us to go to Him in prayer and let our request and needs be made known to Him.

Craft—Verse Frame

Getting It Together

Foam stickers
Glue

Per student:
1 craft verse template from the Ministry Resource CD
4 craft sticks
2 magnets

Putting It Together

1. Print and cut out the Lesson 4 craft verse template.
2. Glue the 4 craft sticks together to make square frame.
3. Glue the craft verse to the back of the craft sticks.
4. Attach the magnets to the back.
5. Decorate the craft sticks with foam stickers, crayons, or markers.

Seeing It Together

Encourage the students to hang this frame in their rooms or on their doors and review the verse every day.

 # Additional Resources

Find the following items on the Ministry Resource CD:

*   Coloring Page (for younger children)
*   Activity Page (for older children)
*   Student Take-Home Paper
*   PowerPoint Presentation

Suggested Classroom Schedule

Before Class	Complete attendance record. Provide students with coloring/activity pages.
Opening	Welcome
Prayer	Prayer requests and praise reports from the children
Song Time	
Memory Verse	James 1:17
Song Time	
Object Lesson	Needs vs. Wants
Bible Lesson	The Foolish Rich Man
Application/Invitation	Help saved students apply lesson. Invite unsaved students to receive Christ.
Snack	Fruit Cups
Review Game/Questions	Balloon Pop
Craft	Hot Air Balloon
Closing	Give announcements and pray. Distribute take home-papers.

Lesson Five Overview

The Foolish Rich Man

Theme—Everything comes from God.

Scripture
Luke 12:16–21

Memory Verse
James 1:17—*"Every good gift and every perfect gift is from above, and cometh down from the Father of lights, with whom is no variableness, neither shadow of turning."*

Lesson Outline

Introducing the Story *(1 Timothy 6:10–11)*

In today's lesson, Jesus tells a story about a man who cared more for his farm than anything else. Jesus reminds us of how important it is to live for God.

Telling the Story

1. **A Big Harvest** *(v. 16, Psalm 50:14)—Flash Card 5.1*

2. **The Farmer's Problem** *(v. 17, Deuteronomy 6:12)*

3. **The Farmer's Solution** *(vv. 18–19)—Flash Card 5.2*

4. **God's Response** *(vv. 20–21, Proverbs 14:12)—Flash Card 5.3*

Applying the Story *(1 John 2:15, Psalm 68:19)*

Jesus told us the story of the rich farmer so we would realize that money is not the most important thing in life. What are you giving your time and money to?

5 Lesson Five

The Foolish Rich Man

Theme: Everything comes from God.

 ## Scripture

Luke 12:16–21

16   And he spake a parable unto them, saying, The ground of a certain rich man brought forth plentifully:

17   And he thought within himself, saying, What shall I do, because I have no room where to bestow my fruits?

18   And he said, This will I do: I will pull down my barns, and build greater; and there will I bestow all my fruits and my goods.

19   And I will say to my soul, Soul, thou hast much goods laid up for many years; take thine ease, eat, drink, and be merry.

20   But God said unto him, Thou fool, this night thy soul shall be required of thee: then whose shall those things be, which thou hast provided?

21   So is he that layeth up treasure for himself, and is not rich toward God.

Teacher's Checklist

❑ Read Luke 12:16–21 daily.

❑ Study Lesson 5.

❑ Flash cards 5.1–5.3

❑ Gather for lesson—2 pitchers, water, cups.

❑ Prepare snack—fruit cups.

❑ Gather for review game—balloons, points page (from the Ministry Resource CD).

❑ Print memory verse visual from the Ministry Resource CD.

❑ Gather for object lesson—various magazines, poster board with titles.

❑ Purchase for craft—1 magnet per student.

❑ Gather for craft—yarn, hole punch, scissors, crayons.

❑ Print craft verse template from the Ministry Resource CD (one per student).

❑ Print and duplicate Coloring Pages or Activity Pages on the Ministry Resource CD (one per student).

❑ Print and duplicate Take-Home Paper on the Ministry Resource CD (one per student).

Snack Suggestion

Consider serving fruit cups. As the children eat the fruit, remind them that everything comes from God.

Bible Lesson

Scripture: Luke 12:16–21

INTRODUCING THE STORY

Have you ever been in a crowd of people at a parade, a ball game, or a pep rally? (Allow time for students to answer.) Then you know what it's like to be in a crowd where the people around you are so tall that you can't see anything except the people right next to you. You know how it is—you stand on your tiptoes and maybe jump a little in hopes of seeing what is going on at the front of the crowd. Sometimes the crowd is so big and so crowded that people step on each other and trip over each other, and you have to make yourself all scrunched up so no one steps on you.

Jesus was speaking to a great crowd of people just like that. There were so many people that no one could count them. Everyone was trying to see Jesus, and they were all stepping on each other as each person tried to get to the front so they could get a better look at Him.

The people in this crowd were people just like you and me, and Jesus was talking about something that was extremely important to each of them. No wonder everyone wanted to get to the front!

Jesus was telling the people how important they were to God. He told the crowd to look at the sparrows. You could buy five sparrows for very little money. Sparrows are not worth much to people, but they are important to God. God knows about each sparrow—He doesn't forget about a single one of them. But you are more important to God than many sparrows. In fact, you are so important God knows everything about you. He even knows how many hairs are on your head! If God takes care of sparrows (and He does), He will take care of you. God will never forget about you (Luke 12:6–7).

Jesus taught this crowd of people about God's great care for us, and He went on to tell them how important it is for us to live for God. Then, right in the middle of Jesus' teaching, a man in that enormous crowd of people called out to Jesus, "Master, speak to my brother, that he divide the inheritance with me" (Luke 12:13). The man didn't seem to care about what Jesus was saying—he just cared that he would get the money he thought he deserved. Can you imagine that? He hollered out in this big crowd of people to ask Jesus something totally different than what Jesus was talking about. He wanted Jesus to tell his brother to be sure to give him a good part of his parents' money.

This man who called to Jesus wanted Him to speak to his brother. He wanted Jesus to say to his brother, "Now, you need to share with your brother all the possessions your father owned before he died. You need to be fair about this. Make sure your brother gets his part. Don't keep everything for yourself."

Jesus gave the man an interesting answer, and His answer led to a story.

1 Timothy 6:10–11

10   *For the love of money is the root of all evil: which while some coveted after, they have erred from the faith, and pierced themselves through with many sorrows.*

11   *But thou, O man of God, flee these things; and follow after righteousness, godliness, faith, love, patience, meekness.*

THE STORY

1. A Big Harvest (v. 16)

Flash Card 5.1

There was once a farmer who dearly loved his farm. He loved his farm so much that he worked from morning 'til night on his farm. He loved his farm so much that he taught his sons how to do the farm work so they could have farms of their own some day. He loved his farm so much that he bought more and more land and hired more and more servants to help him take care of his enormous farm.

The farmer became very proud of his farm. When friends would come to visit, he would say, "Let me take you to my fields and show you the amazing crops I am growing this year. Let me take you to my barns and show you all the grain I have stored up to feed my animals. Let me take you to my pastures and show you all the sheep and cows I have raised."

When he returned to his house each evening, he didn't have time to talk to his wife. He didn't have time to play with his children. He didn't have time to read his Bible or pray. He was too busy thinking about the next day's work, how much he would charge people to buy his grain, and what abundant crops he was growing in his fields. As he lay down to sleep at night, he would think about what a fine farmer he was until he drifted off to sleep.

The farmer loved his farm so much that he forgot the one who gave him his farm. He forgot who gave him the air he breathed and the strength he needed in order to do his work. He forgot who created the ground where he planted his crops. He forgot who formed the seed from which each of his millions of plants grew. He forgot who sent the rain and sunshine to cause the crops to grow. He forgot to thank God for the many blessings on his farm.

Psalm 50:14

14   *Offer unto God thanksgiving; and pay thy vows unto the most High.*

In the mornings, the farmer didn't eat breakfast with his family. He ate his food alone and quickly hurried out the door. The farmer saw his hard work turn out even better than he had hoped—he had beautiful crops of fruit and grain. He had such abundant crops, in fact, that he didn't have enough room in his barns to hold all of it.

2. The Farmer's Problem (v. 17)

The farmer thought to himself, "What shall I do, because I have no room where to bestow my fruits?" (Luke 12:17). He didn't know what to do with all his grain—there was too much to fit into his barns! And, forgetting who had given him all the grain, the farmer felt very proud of himself. It was wonderful, the farmer thought, to have so much grain that he didn't have room in his barns to store it.

Deuteronomy 6:12

12   *Then beware lest thou forget the LORD, which brought thee forth out of the land of Egypt, from the house of bondage.*

3. The Farmer's Solution (vv. 18–19)

Flash Card 5.2

Then, the farmer said, "This will I do: I will pull down my barns, and build greater; and there will I bestow all my fruits and my goods" (Luke 12:18). "I have an idea: I'll tear down the small barns I have, and I will build bigger barns. Then I'll have room to store all the things I have grown on my land." And the farmer felt very proud of himself for having such a grand idea. The farmer didn't think about asking God what he should do with the extra grain that was too much to fit into his barns. The farmer didn't think about giving some of his grain to God who had given him so much. The farmer still forgot who had given him his farm and his crops and everything he owned.

Finally, the farmer said, "I will say to my soul, Soul, thou hast much goods laid up for many years; take thine ease, eat, drink, and be merry" (Luke 12:19). "After I have pulled down my barns, after I have built bigger barns, after I have stored my fruit and grains and equipment in my barns, life will be so easy. I will talk to myself. I'll say, 'Self, you have done such an amazing job. You have stored up all the food you will need for a long time—many years, in fact. It's time for you to take it easy. Just eat, drink, and have a good time—you deserve it.'" And the farmer still forgot about God.

4. God's Response (vv. 20–21)

Flash Card 5.3

But the farmer didn't forget about God for long, because God spoke to him. God said, "You have been so foolish. Life isn't going to go on the way you have planned. Tonight you are going to die. Now, I have something for you to think about: When you die, who will own all the things you are planning on storing in your big barns? Who will own your grain? Who will own your horses and wagons? Who will own your house and your barns? They will belong to someone else—you won't be here to enjoy them" (from Luke 12:20).

That's not all God said to the proud farmer. God said, "So is he that layeth up treasure for himself, and is not rich toward God" (Luke 12:21). God explained that what was about to happen to the farmer was what happens to everyone like him. Each person who spends his life working to get things for himself and forgets about God will end up just like the proud farmer. He will die, and his things will be owned by someone else. He will not have the peace in his heart that comes from being grateful to God for all the things He has given him. He will not have the joy in his heart that comes from loving others and sharing the gifts God has given him. He will die, selfish and disappointed with life.

Proverbs 14:12

12   There is a way which seemeth right unto a man, but the end
     thereof are the ways of death.

APPLYING THE STORY

After Jesus told this parable (story), He knew the people would be wondering how they could be rich toward God. Jesus knew the people would be wondering how they could keep from becoming like the rich farmer—selfish and full of pride. So, Jesus gave them some very important instructions, and Jesus' words were for each of us here in this room, as well.

Jesus told the crowd to not spend their time thinking about themselves. There is something more important than what you are going to eat. There is something more important than what you are going to drink. There is something more important than what you are going to wear.

1 John 2:15

15   Love not the world, neither the things that are in the world.
     If any man love the world, the love of the Father is not
     in him.

Jesus said, "I want you to look at the birds. They don't plant crops like the farmer did, they don't harvest crops like the farmer did, and they don't have barns to hold their crops like the farmer did. But God feeds them! They have just what they need. You are so much more important to God than birds" (from Luke 12:22–24).

"Look at yourself," Jesus said. "No matter how hard you try, you cannot make yourself taller. If you stand on your tiptoes or wear high heeled shoes, you might look taller, but you are not actually taller. There is nothing you can do to make yourself taller—God takes care of that. Since God is the one who takes care of something as simple as making you taller, you can trust Him to take care of all of the needs you have in your life" (from Luke 12:25–26).

"Think about the flowers," Jesus continued. "They don't work in the cotton fields, growing cotton to weave into fabric. They don't spin wool into yarn to knit warm sweaters. They don't sew silk into beautiful clothing. But God clothes them! God gives the flowers clothes that are more beautiful than Solomon's—the richest king who ever lived! If God gives the flowers, that live for such a short time, clothes more beautiful than a king, you can be sure He will give you the clothes you need. You are so much more important to God than flowers" (from Luke 12:27–28).

So you don't need to worry about what you will eat, drink, or wear. People who don't know the great God who created them and everything else in the world worry about those things. But Christians know God will take care of them.

Psalm 68:19

19   *Blessed be the Lord, who daily loadeth us with benefits,*
      even the God of our salvation. Selah

Instead of thinking about food and clothes, think about God. Think about how much He has given you. Thank Him for His gifts to you. Give God back some of the gifts He has given to you. Give money in the offering. Share some of what God has given to you with someone who doesn't have as much as you do.

"For where your treasure is, there will your heart be also" (Luke 12:34). When you give to God, you will love Him more. When you give to people who have needs, you will love them more. Who—or what you give to, you will love.

What can you give?

- You can give your time reading the Bible, praying, and witnessing to others.
- Do chores for your parents or teacher with a cheerful heart.
- Play with a little sister/brother when you would rather do something for yourself.
- Write a thank you note to someone instead of watching television.
- Rake leaves or mow the lawn for an elderly person, without charging them.
- Spend time with a classmate who doesn't have many friends.
- Write a letter to your grandparents.
- Give money in the offering plate in Sunday school and church.
- Give money to a missionary, rather than buying yourself a soda or candy bar.

- Save to buy a jacket or pair of shoes for a classmate whose jacket or shoes have holes.
- Buy your mother or grandmother a flower for her table. (Ask students for their ideas.)

Jesus told the story of the rich farmer to the man who asked Him to tell his brother to divide the inheritance with him. Jesus told the story of the rich farmer to the rest of the people in the great crowd that day. And Jesus told the story of the rich farmer to you and to me. He wanted us to know that money is not what is really important in life, and He wanted to teach us that God, who feeds the birds and clothes the flowers, will take care of us, too.

Review Game/Questions

Balloon Pop

Materials Needed

- Balloons
- Points from the Ministry Resource CD

Instructions

Print out and cut points. Roll the points into a cylinder and place in a deflated balloon. Inflate the balloon and knot the end.

Divide class into teams. After answering a review question correctly, students may choose a balloon. They may pop the balloon and retrieve the points. Award the team the points and repeat with the next team. The team with the most points wins.

1. Who does everything come from?
    Answer: God

2. Name a word that describes the farmer in our story.
    Answer: Prideful, selfish, greedy

3. What was the most important thing to this proud farmer?
    Answer: His farm, his riches

4. The farmer had such a large harvest, that he made a plan to store all of his grain. What was the plan?
    Answer: To tear down his barns and build bigger ones

5. In all of his dreams and plans, whom did the greedy farmer forget?
    Answer: God

6. What did God tell the farmer?
    Answer: He was a fool, and he would die.

7. What does God tell us not to be concerned with?
    Answer: Our possessions on earth

8. Instead of thinking about our food and clothes, what should we think about?
    Answer: God and giving to others

9. What are some ways you can give to others?

    Answer: Answers will vary, but may include the examples given on page 76.

10. Name some ways God has given to you.

    Answer: Answers will vary but may include family, church, home, food, friends, etc.

 ## Teaching the Memory Verse

James 1:17

17 Every good gift and every perfect gift is from above, and cometh down from the Father of lights, with whom is no variableness, neither shadow of turning.

Print memory verse from the Ministry Resource CD onto cardstock. Have students open their Bibles to James 1:17. Read the verse several times in phrases. Also, emphasize a new word each time you read it. Then show the class the flash card. Have class recite the verse. Now, using the second flash card, challenge the students to see if they can say the verse without the help of any vowels.

Object Lesson—Needs vs. Wants

Needs vs. Wants Collages:

Have children cut out magazine pictures of various objects. Instruct the children to work with their table or small group to glue pictures on a large piece of poster board divided into two columns titled "Needs" and "Wants." If you do not have time for the children to cut these pictures, you could already have pictures ready before class (either from a magazine or printed from your computer).

Discussion Questions:

What is a "need"? What is a "want"? What is the difference? Is it okay to get things we want? Are there people who don't have their "needs"? I wonder how God feels about people's needs and wants? How can we help make sure everyone's needs are met? Who supplies all of our wants and needs?

Additional Resources

Find the following items on the Ministry Resource CD:

- Coloring Page (for younger children)
- Activity Page (for older children)
- Student Take-Home Paper
- PowerPoint Presentation

Craft—Hot Air Balloon

Getting It Together

Yarn
Hole Punch
Scissors
Crayons

Per student:

1   magnet
1   verse template located on the Ministry Resource CD

Putting It Together

1. Print and cut out the Lesson 5 craft template.
2. Have the students color the hot air balloon.
3. Hole punch the bottom of the balloon.
4. Put two hole punches on the basket (one on each side).
5. Attach the basket of the hot air balloon by stringing yarn from the bottom of the hot air balloon to the two holes in the basket.
6. Attach a magnet to the back of the balloon.

Seeing It Together

Remind students that everything they have is from God above.

Suggested Classroom Schedule

Before Class	Complete attendance record. Provide students with coloring/activity pages.	
Opening	Welcome	
Prayer	Prayer requests and praise reports from the children	
Song Time		
Memory Verse	John 14:6	
Song Time		
Object Lesson	God Knows You!	
Bible Lesson	The Good Shepherd	
Application/Invitation	Help saved students apply lesson. Invite unsaved students to receive Christ.	
Snack	Popcorn Ball "Sheep"	
Review Game/Questions	The Way	
Craft	Shepherd	
Closing	Give announcements and pray. Distribute take-home papers.	

Lesson Six Overview

The Good Shepherd
Theme—Jesus is the Chief Shepherd.

Scripture
John 10:1–17

Memory Verse
John 14:6—"Jesus saith unto him, I am the way, the truth, and the life: no man cometh unto the Father, but by me."

Lesson Outline
Introducing the Story
In today's story, Jesus tells a story about a shepherd and his sheep. The crowd of people listening did not believe Jesus was who He said He was. Jesus told this story to help them understand.

Telling the Story
1. **The Shepherd and the Sheepfold** —Flash Card 6.1
2. **A Thief Enters the Sheepfold** (v. 1)
3. **The Good Shepherd Enters the Sheepfold** (vv. 2–4) —Flash Card 6.2
4. **Sheep Won't Follow a Stranger** (v. 5)

Jesus Explains the Story (John 14:6, Psalm 16:11, Hebrews 13:5b, Romans 10:17)—Flash Card 6.3
Jesus explains why we are like His sheep; He is our Shepherd.

Applying the Story (2 Corinthians 11:3, Acts 20:29, 1 Peter 5:8)
If you have trusted Jesus as your Saviour, then you have gone through the one door that will take you to Heaven. If you have not yet gone through that door,

6 Lesson Six

The Good Shepherd

Theme: Jesus is the Chief Shepherd.

Scripture

John 10:1–17

1   Verily, verily, I say unto you, He that entereth not by the door into the sheepfold, but climbeth up some other way, the same is a thief and a robber.

2   But he that entereth in by the door is the shepherd of the sheep.

3   To him the porter openeth; and the sheep hear his voice: and he calleth his own sheep by name, and leadeth them out.

4   And when he putteth forth his own sheep, he goeth before them, and the sheep follow him: for they know his voice.

5   And a stranger will they not follow, but will flee from him: for they know not the voice of strangers.

6   This parable spake Jesus unto them: but they understood not what things they were which he spake unto them.

7   Then said Jesus unto them again, Verily, verily, I say unto you, I am the door of the sheep.

8   All that ever came before me are thieves and robbers: but the sheep did not hear them.

9   I am the door: by me if any man enter in, he shall be saved, and shall go in and out, and find pasture.

10 The thief cometh not, but for to steal, and to kill, and to destroy: I am come that they might have life, and that they might have it more abundantly.

11 I am the good shepherd: the good shepherd giveth his life for the sheep.

12 But he that is an hireling, and not the shepherd, whose own the sheep are not, seeth the wolf coming, and leaveth the sheep, and fleeth: and the wolf catcheth them, and scattereth the sheep.

13 The hireling fleeth, because he is an hireling, and careth not for the sheep.

> **Memory Verse**
>
> **John 14:6**
> "Jesus saith unto him, I am the way, the truth, and the life: no man cometh unto the Father, but by me."

14 *I am the good shepherd, and know my sheep, and am known of mine.*

15 *As the Father knoweth me, even so know I the Father: and I lay down my life for the sheep.*

16 *And other sheep I have, which are not of this fold: them also I must bring, and they shall hear my voice; and there shall be one fold, and one shepherd.*

17 *Therefore doth my Father love me, because I lay down my life, that I might take it again.*

Teacher's Checklist

❑   Read John 10:1–17 daily.

❑   Study Lesson 6.

❑   Flash cards 6.1–6.3

❑   Prepare snack—popcorn balls and candy for sheep faces.

❑   Gather for lesson—blades of grass or plant, water, robe, headdress and stick for shepherd, magnets.

❑   Gather for object lesson—a dozen eggs (one hard-boiled).

❑   Print game card pieces from the Ministry Resource CD.

❑   Purchase for craft (per student)—light brown chenille, hair colored chenille, 1 rubber band, 1 styrofoam cup, 2 craft eyes.

❑   Print Lesson 6 craft verse template from the Ministry Resource CD (one per student).

❑   Gather for craft—foam glue, construction paper, tan cardstock, scissors, fabric.

❑   Print and duplicate Coloring Pages or Activity Pages on the Ministry Resource CD (one per student).

❑   Print and duplicate Take-Home Paper on the Ministry Resource CD (one per student).

Snack Suggestion

Popcorn Ball "Sheep"
Prepare popcorn balls and use candy to make the face of the sheep. Serve the students popcorn balls and remind them of our loving Shepherd.

Bible Lesson

Scripture: John 10:1–17

INTRODUCING THE STORY

If I were to describe something my puppy did this morning, you would understand exactly what I was talking about. You are familiar with puppies, so you would picture her actions in your mind.

If I said, "The moment I opened Lady's crate to take her outside, she tumbled onto the floor and turned somersaults," you would smile as you pictured a wriggly little puppy rolling around on the floor. If I then said, "When I picked her up into my arms, she wriggled and squirmed as she licked my face all over," you would remember a time you have held a squirmy little puppy that licked your face. If I told you, "I set her down on the floor, and as she heard me scooping food out of the dog food bag, she scampered in excited circles around her dish," you would imagine a puppy tumbling and rolling around its dish, eagerly waiting for its food.

Although the puppy illustration would be applicable to any age students, a class with only older students may relate better to an alternate illustration. You could describe a sports event, a cooking procedure, or a youth activity, for example.

If I went on to compare Lady's excitement to how you feel sometimes, you would understand that too. I could say, "You are like that puppy when the bell rings to let you know it's time for recess," and you would know what I mean. You would remember sitting at your desk all morning, quietly doing your work. Your muscles are tired of being still, and they want to move. They want to run and jump and throw a ball or swing on a swing. The moment the bell rings, you stand up, put your books away, and get out the door as soon as you can. You run to the swings, grab a ball and start bouncing it, or you find a few friends and play tag. It feels good to be able to move again.

Or, if I said, "That's what you are like when your mom says, 'There's ice cream for dessert', " you would understand. You would picture yourself excited about the ice cream, just like the puppy was excited when it knew its food was on the way.

Jesus, also, told stories that related to things with which people of His day were very familiar. One of His favorite characters to use was sheep, because so many people were shepherds. Jesus' listeners understood the habits and characteristics of sheep and shepherds. Jesus said people are like sheep.

When Jesus talked about sheep, the people listening to Him knew a lot about sheep.

- Sheep know the sound of their own shepherd's voice, and they won't follow another voice.
- Sheep are often attacked by other animals—dogs, bears, and/or coyotes.
- Sheep are often stolen by rustlers (people who steal cattle or sheep).
- Sheep are fearful animals. If they are attacked, they will do one of three things: huddle into little groups, simply stand there, alone and frozen with fear, or run.
- Sheep depend on their shepherd for everything. They need the shepherd to lead them to fresh water and fresh grass.
- Sheep can't make decisions on their own.
- Sheep don't know what is good for them. They don't know what plants are poisonous for them and which ones are not.
- Sheep are stubborn.
- At night, sheep are taken to a closed-in place, called a fold, to keep them safe.
- Sometimes a sheep will turn over on its back and not be able to get up again. This is called a "cast" sheep. A cast sheep needs its shepherd to turn it onto its feet again.

Jesus' listeners also knew a lot about good shepherds.

- A good shepherd makes sure his sheep have clean water every day.
- A good shepherd leads his sheep to fresh pasture (grass).
- A good shepherd will do whatever it takes to protect his sheep from wild animals or thieves that would hurt or steal his sheep.
- A good shepherd will even give his life, if need be, to protect his sheep.
- A good shepherd examines his sheep to make sure they are not sick and that they don't have wounds hidden under their thick wool.
- A good shepherd will bring his sheep into the safety of the fold every night. He will watch so that no person or animal sneaks in over the wall to steal or harm his sheep.
- A good shepherd keeps his sheep safe from dangerous weather, like hail or tornadoes.
- A good shepherd is gentle and kind to his sheep.
- A good shepherd knows each of his sheep.

    The Stories of Our Saviour | © 2011 Striving Together Publications

Jesus told a story about a shepherd and his sheep to a group of people. These people didn't believe Jesus was who He said He was. So Jesus told this story to help them understand.

THE STORY
1. The Shepherd and the Sheepfold

There once was a shepherd boy. Each day, at sunup, his father would send him out to the pasture with the flocks of sheep. There the sheep could eat the crisp, green grass and drink the dew that sparkled on the grass in the early morning hours. The shepherd boy would follow his father's instructions and lead his sheep to the best and freshest pastures. Sometimes a lion or bear would creep near his sheep, trying to get one of them, and the shepherd boy would chase him away with his shepherd's rod. This hard-working shepherd boy spent all day out with the flocks, and he led them home to the sheepfold in the evening, before dark.

As the shepherd boy grew, he realized he loved being a shepherd. He loved going to the sheepfold early in the morning and rattling the door of the sheepfold. He loved whistling and singing and calling to his sheep before he went into the sheepfold, so they would recognize him and not be afraid. He loved his sheep, and he loved taking care of them and protecting them. He loved keeping a sharp eye out for those who would hurt his sheep. He loved caring for his sheep's wounds and giving them medicine when they were sick. He loved how his sheep came to him when they heard his voice. He loved each sheep, he knew all their names, and he called each one by its name.

When the shepherd boy was grown and had a family of his own, he became the shepherd. He wasn't just a shepherd boy anymore. He was a full-fledged shepherd—a good shepherd. Just as he had done when he was a boy, the good shepherd took excellent care of his sheep.

2. A Thief Enters the Sheepfold (v. 1)

Every night the shepherd would stand at the door of the sheepfold and count each sheep as it walked into the fold. He would rub his hands through

Teaching Tip

Bring a few blades of grass or a plant to class. Sprinkle droplets of water onto the leaves to show the students "dew."

Flash Card 6.1

Act It Out

Shepherd
Dress up in a shepherd's costume—robe and headdress. Hold a staff (A long, heavy stick will do.) As you tell the story of the Good Shepherd, act the part of a shepherd. Gently take a student's arm as you speak of examining a sheep for injuries. Call the names of your students as you tell of the shepherd calling his sheep by name. Hold a stuffed sheep in your arms throughout the lesson.

Flash Card 6.2

and underneath the wool of each sheep so he could feel if the sheep had any cuts or other injuries. Then he would lock the door of the sheepfold and leave the porter (someone in charge of the door and the keys) to watch the door of the sheepfold through the night.

But some nights, after the good shepherd led his sheep home to the fold, things did not go as they should. Sometimes someone else would try to get into the sheepfold—someone who didn't belong there. This man never rattled the door and called to the sheep as he came up to the sheepfold. This man never whistled or sang to let the sheep know all was safe. This man never went to the porter and asked him to open the door. This man was a thief and a robber. He never entered the sheepfold through the door. He would enter the sheepfold by sneaking over the wall so he could steal and kill some of the good shepherd's sheep.

The sheep would run, bleating (the "baa" sound a sheep makes), to the sides of the sheepfold, trying to escape from the thief. The porter would call the shepherd so he could protect his sheep from the thief.

3. The Good Shepherd Enters the Sheepfold (vv. 2–4)

Most of the time, things went well for the shepherd and his sheep. When the good shepherd came to the door of the sheepfold, he always sang. He always whistled and called out to the sheep. The porter gladly opened the door for the good shepherd. The sheep crowded around the good shepherd as he called each one by its name and led them out to the pasture.

The good shepherd never sent his sheep out to the pasture. They wouldn't know how to go there alone. They wouldn't know how to take care of themselves. They wouldn't know which grass would make them healthy. They might eat something that would make them sick. They might get attacked by wild animals. The shepherd loved his sheep, and he would never send them out ahead of him. The shepherd went ahead of his sheep, and he gently led his sheep as they followed his voice.

The sheep gladly followed the kind and gentle good shepherd. He talked and sang to them, and they loved to hear his voice. They trusted the voice of the good shepherd.

88   **The Stories of Our Saviour** | © 2011 Striving Together Publications

4. Sheep Won't Follow a Stranger (v. 5)

Sometimes a stranger would try to call the sheep away from the good shepherd. The stranger would whistle and sing and talk to the sheep the same way the shepherd did, but the sheep knew it was a different voice. The sheep didn't trust the voice of a stranger, and they ran away from his voice.

JESUS EXPLAINS THE STORY

The people who were listening to the story about the good shepherd and the sheep understood all the things that Jesus said about the sheep and about the shepherd. They were familiar with sheep, and they often saw sheep with their shepherds. But they didn't understand why Jesus told the story, and they didn't see what they should learn from it. So Jesus explained.

"I am the door," said Jesus. "By me if any man enter in, he shall be saved" (John 10:9a). Jesus told the people that He was the only way to Heaven.

John 14:6

6   I am the way, the truth, and the life: no man cometh unto
       the Father, but by me.

Just as sheep need to go through the door of the sheepfold in order to enter it, the only way a person can go to Heaven is through the door— Jesus Christ.

Flash Card 6.3

Jesus said, "All that ever came before me were thieves and robbers" (John 10:8). Thieves and robbers have come and tried to tell people there are other ways to Heaven. They are not there to help the sheep, but "to steal, and to kill, and to destroy" (John 10:10a). They will destroy the most valuable thing a person has—his soul. The soul is the part of a person that will live forever, and the thief would like to keep a person's soul from going to Heaven.

Jesus said, "I am the good shepherd: the good shepherd giveth his life for the sheep" (John 10:11). Someone's life had to be given in order for a person to go to Heaven, because Romans 6:23a says, "the wages of sin is death." Wages are what we earn for what we do; and what we earn for our sin is death. If we died without having our sin paid for, we would not be able to go to Heaven—we would have to pay for our sins forever in the place the Bible calls the Lake of Fire.

But Jesus gave His life for us. Jesus died to make the payment of death for our sins so we wouldn't have to. His payment of death makes Him our door (and the only door) to Heaven.

Then, Jesus said that those who are saved—those who have entered through the door—will "go in and out, and find pasture" (John 10:9b). Pasture for sheep is just what they need in order to grow and be happy. Sheep who are led by their shepherd to green pastures in the morning and back to the sheepfold at night are the happiest sheep there are. They have everything they need, and their good shepherd takes care of them. They belong to the shepherd, and they are happy and protected under his care.

Psalm 16:11

11 *Thou wilt shew me the path of life: in thy presence is fullness of joy; at thy right hand there are pleasures for evermore.*

Jesus said that, while the thief comes to steal and kill and destroy, "I am come that they might have life, and that they might have it more abundantly" (John 10:10).

- The thief steals our happiness, but Jesus gives joy and peace.
- The thief kills our souls, but Jesus gives eternal life.
- The thief destroys our lives, but Jesus gives lives full of all good things.

There are people in this world who take care of sheep, but they don't love the sheep. They aren't true shepherds. They don't really care about the sheep, because the sheep don't belong to them. They just go from shepherd to shepherd, hiring themselves out to help take care of the sheep until they earn enough money to move on. Jesus called them hirelings, and they're different than real shepherds.

When a hireling sees a wolf coming, he runs away, because he doesn't care about the sheep. The hireling leaves the sheep to take care of himself when he is in danger—just when the sheep need him the most! The wolf catches some of the sheep and kills them, and the rest of the flock is scattered, and the sheep have to try to take care of themselves.

"But I," Jesus said, "am the good shepherd, and know my sheep, and am known of mine…I lay down my life for the sheep" (John 10:14, 15b). Jesus said that even though there are hirelings who will leave their sheep when the sheep are in danger, Jesus is always there to care for His sheep. He is not afraid of danger, and He never leaves His sheep to take care of themselves.

Hebrews 13:5b

5b   *I will never leave thee, nor forsake thee.*

Jesus wanted us to know that He still has other sheep who are not saved yet. They need to hear His voice.

Romans 10:17

17   *So then faith cometh by hearing, and hearing by the word of God.*

These sheep need to hear the Shepherd's voice so they can enter in through the door and be saved.

APPLYING THE STORY

Have you ever heard a preacher or teacher say that there are many ways to Heaven? Some people say you can go to Heaven by doing good works. Some people say you can go to Heaven by going to church. Some people say you can go to Heaven by being baptized or taking the Lord's Supper. Some people say you can go to Heaven by giving money in the offering or by confessing your sins to a church leader. Some people say there are many doors that lead to Heaven.

2 Corinthians 11:3

3   *But I fear, lest by any means, as the serpent beguiled Eve through his subtilty, so your minds should be corrupted from the simplicity that is in Christ.*

But, that is not what Jesus said. Jesus said there is only one way to Heaven, and that is through Him. People who say there are other doors to Heaven are like the thieves and the robbers in Jesus' parable (story) about the Good Shepherd. The words they speak are not true, and if we believe them, our lives will be destroyed.

Use an Object

Magnet of Jesus
Use magnets to show how the sheep hear the Shepherd's voice. Demonstrate this by joining the positive and negative ends of the magnets. Magnets will "stick" together. We will be safe when we follow our Saviour. Show the opposite effect. If we want to go our own way, we will leave our Saviour. Join the positive ends of your magnets. They will repel.

Acts 20:29

29   For I know this, that after my departing shall grievous
wolves enter in among you, not sparing the flock.

If you have trusted Jesus as your Saviour from sin, then you have gone through the one door that will take you to Heaven. If you have not yet gone through that door, you can do so today! Talk with one of the teachers after class, and we will be happy to show you how you can trust Jesus as your Saviour and have a home in Heaven forever.

Many of you are sheep who have gone through the door of Jesus and trusted Him as your only way to Heaven. Jesus told this story to remind you to follow the Good Shepherd. He wants you to know that your Good Shepherd:

- will provide everything you need.
- will do whatever it takes to protect you from your enemy, Satan, who would like to steal your joy and keep you from having a good life.
- gave His life for you.
- will examine your heart to make sure it is right with Him.
- will watch over you so no enemy will sneak in to harm you.
- is kind and gentle.
- knows you by name.
- loves you.
- will never leave you and will never forsake you.

There is a thief, Satan, who would like to destroy your life. He is like a wolf or a lion that tries to sneak into the sheepfold. He desires to harm you. He doesn't tell you he wants to hurt you. He disguises himself to make you think he is going to make your life happier and better.

1 Peter 5:8

8   Be sober, be vigilant; because your adversary the devil, as a
roaring lion, walketh about, seeking whom he may devour.

- He might sneak into your life through your friend who coaxes you to steal so you can have that piece of candy or that cap you wished for.
- He might sneak into your life through the temptation to be jealous when someone gets an award you had tried to earn.

- He might sneak into your life through the temptation to not read your Bible or pray.
- He might sneak into your life through the temptation to get back at your brother or sister who said something mean or unkind to you.
- He might sneak into your life through the temptation to lie to your parents.
- He might sneak into your life by telling you in your mind that God doesn't really love you.
- He might sneak into your life through the temptation to sleep in when it's time for Sunday school and church.
- He might sneak into your life through the temptation to not listen during the times your Good Shepherd is speaking to you—a sermon in church, a lesson in Sunday school, or during your Bible reading time. When are other times the Good Shepherd tries to speak to us?

The Good Shepherd knows how to take care of you—His sheep. He knows your name, and He knows everything about you. He knows exactly what you need, and He wants to give it to you. He wants you to trust Him and to know the gentle, tender love of your Good Shepherd.

You will be under the protection of your Good Shepherd as long as you follow His voice. You hear His voice through reading His Word. You hear His voice through the preaching at church. You hear His voice through the teaching in Sunday school. You hear His voice through other people who love Him and live for Him. He will care for you—all you have to do is follow.

Review Game/Questions

The Way

Materials Needed

Game pieces from the Ministry Resource CD

Instructions

Print and cut games pieces. The Cross goes behind one of the game pieces. Laminate for durability.

Place game pieces in a pocket chart. Ask a review question. If the student answers correctly, allow him to come to the board and pick one of "The Way" cards. If he finds the card with the Cross on the back he gets a piece of candy. Continue asking questions until the Cross is found. If the Cross is found right away, shuffle the cards and play again.

1. Name some characteristics of sheep.
   Answer: See page 86.

2. Name some characteristics of a good shepherd.
   Answer: See page 86.

3. What do sheep know about the shepherd?
   Answer: Sheep know the shepherd's voice. They know he will lead them.

4. What would a good shepherd do every night when the sheep entered the fold?
   Answer: He would count the sheep and make sure they were okay.

5. Who would sometimes try to enter the sheepfold (who didn't belong there)?
   Answer: A thief or robber

6. Who is like a wolf or lion who tries to destroy you?
   Answer: Satan

7. What are some ways our adversary, the devil, might try to hurt or harm us?
   Answer: See examples on pages 92 and 93.

8. Who is our Good Shepherd?
   Answer: God

9. Name some characteristics of our Good Shepherd.
   Answer: See characteristics on page 92.

10. Who is the Door, the only way, to Heaven?
    Answer: Jesus

 # Teaching the Memory Verse

John 14:6

6   *Jesus saith unto him, I am the way, the truth, and the life: no man cometh unto the Father, but by me.*

Have students open their Bibles to John 14:6. If you have a red letter Bible, you will see this verse is in red, because this is Jesus speaking. He is proclaiming that the only way to God the Father is through Jesus. Anyone who says that there are other ways to Heaven is lying.

Divide the class into two teams. Have them stand in a line, the leaders of each line facing each other. Instruct students to say the verse in a ping pong style. The first person on Team 1 says "John 14:6," and goes to the end of the line. Then the first person on Team 2 says "Jesus," and goes to the end of the line; the first person on Team 1 now says "saith" and goes to the end of the line. Keep repeating the process with the rest of the verse. The first few times allow students to use their Bibles. After the class has a good grasp of the verse, they will play again without using their Bibles. If a student misses the word they were to say, they must sit down.

Object Lesson—God Knows You!

Materials Needed:
A dozen eggs

For the Teacher:
From the egg carton, choose one egg and boil it for ten minutes. The other eleven eggs will remain raw. Put all twelve eggs in the carton on the display table (there is no need to mark the hard-boiled egg).

To the Class:
John 10:14 says, "I am the good shepherd, and **know** my sheep, and am known of mine" (emphasis added). Can any of you tell me which egg is different from the others in this carton? They all look the same, don't they? The difference is not on the outside of the egg but on the inside.

Jesus knows our hearts! He knows whether or not we really are truly saved. There are many in the world today who look and even act like a Christian but have never accepted Christ as their Saviour. Jesus knows His sheep and knows if they have accepted Him.

Jesus not only knows if we are saved, He know everything about us that no one else sees! He knows our thoughts, feelings, fears, and hopes! And He loves us just like a shepherd loves his sheep! (Let a child come to the front and try to find the boiled egg.)

It can be very difficult to find the egg that is different because they all look alike on the outside. It is important that each one of us knows that Jesus lives in our hearts and realizes that He knows all about us and still loves us!

 # Additional Resources

Find the following items on the Ministry Resource CD:

- Coloring Page (for younger children)
- Activity Page (for older children)
- Student Take-Home Paper
- PowerPoint Presentation

Craft—Shepherd

Getting It Together

Foam glue
Construction paper
Fabric
Tan cardstock
Scissors

Per student:
Lesson 6 craft verse template
Light brown chenille
Hair colored chenille
1 small rubber band
Styrofoam cup
2 craft eyes

Putting It Together

1. Print and cut out the Lesson 6 craft template from the Ministry Resource CD.
2. Curl the ends of the verse to make it look like an opened scroll.
3. Make a shepherd's staff out of the light brown chenille.
4. Glue cardstock around the cup to resemble the shepherd's outfit, leaving about an inch of the cup showing to make the face.
5. Glue on the eyes and draw a mouth.
6. Cut the hair colored chenille into 2 inch strips, poke them through the bottom of the cup, forming hair.
7. Cut strips of fabric putting it over the hair, attach with a rubber band.
8. Glue the verse and staff to the cup.

Seeing It Together

This little shepherd can remind us to let Jesus be the Shepherd of our hearts and to let Him guide our lives.

Suggested Classroom Schedule

Before Class	Complete attendance record. Provide students with coloring/activity pages.
Opening	Welcome
Prayer	Prayer requests and praise reports from the children
Song Time	
Memory Verse	John 15:13
Song Time	
Object Lesson	I Lost It!
Bible Lesson	The Lost Sheep
Application/Invitation	Help saved students apply lesson. Invite unsaved students to receive Christ.
Snack	Butterfly Treat
Review Game/Questions	Finding the Lost Sheep
Craft	Sheep
Closing	Give announcements and pray. Distribute take-home papers.

Lesson Seven Overview

The Lost Sheep
Theme—Jesus loves His sheep.

Scripture
Luke 15:1–7

Memory Verse
John 15:13—*"Greater love hath no man than this, that a man lay down his life for his friends."*

Lesson Outline
Introducing the Story *(Luke 19:10)*

Today's story is about how much Jesus cares about each one of us. There were some men called Pharisees who were angry that Jesus cared about everyone. Jesus tells this story to help the Pharisees understand that He wants everyone in Heaven.

Telling the Story
1. **A Shepherd Has One Hundred Sheep** *(John 10:3b, 14)* —*Flash Card 7.1*

2. **A Sheep Is Lost**—*Flash Card 7.2*

3. **The Shepherd Searches for the Lost Sheep**

4. **The Shepherd Finds His Sheep**—*Flash Card 7.3*

5. **The Shepherd Rejoices with His Friends and Neighbors**

Jesus Explains the Story *(Isaiah 53:6, 1 Peter 5:8b, Luke 19:10, John 10:11)*

Applying the Story *(Romans 3:23)*
Every person in the entire world has been lost in their sins and needs to be

7 Lesson Seven

The Lost Sheep

Theme: Jesus loves His sheep.

 ## Scripture

Luke 15:1–7

1   Then drew near unto him all the publicans and sinners for to hear him.
2   And the Pharisees and scribes murmured, saying, This man receiveth sinners, and eateth with them.
3   And he spake this parable unto them, saying,
4   What man of you, having an hundred sheep, if he lose one of them, doth not leave the ninety and nine in the wilderness, and go after that which is lost, until he find it?
5   And when he hath found it, he layeth it on his shoulders, rejoicing.
6   And when he cometh home, he calleth together his friends and neighbours, saying unto them, Rejoice with me; for I have found my sheep which was lost.
7   I say unto you, that likewise joy shall be in heaven over one sinner that repenteth, more than over ninety and nine just persons, which need no repentance.

Memory Verse

John 15:13
"Greater love hath no man than this, that a man lay down his life for his friends."

Teacher's Checklist

 ## Snack Suggestion

Butterfly Treat
Just as the caterpillar changes into a butterfly, when a person is saved, that person becomes a new creature. To make this snack, slightly melt caramel candy on a silicone mat on a cookie sheet. Quickly add two twisty pretzels to form wings and add two chocolate chips for the eyes. For a healthier version: cut celery into approximately two-inch pieces. Fill with cream cheese. Add the pretzels for wings and raisins for eyes.

- ❑ Read Luke 15:1–7 daily.
- ❑ Study Lesson 7.
- ❑ Flash cards 7.1–7.3
- ❑ Gather for lesson—binoculars.
- ❑ Prepare snack—melted caramel candy, pretzels, chocolate chips.
- ❑ Print and cut out game pieces for review game from the Ministry Resource CD.
- ❑ Print this week's memory verse (John 15:13) from the Ministry Resource CD.
- ❑ Gather for object lesson—stuffed animals/toys.
- ❑ Purchase for craft—cotton balls, 1 craft eye per student.
- ❑ Print for craft—verse template from the Ministry Resource CD.
- ❑ Gather for craft—black cardstock, scissors, glue.
- ❑ Print and duplicate Coloring Pages or Activity Pages on the Ministry Resource CD (one per student).
- ❑ Print and duplicate Take-Home Paper on the Ministry Resource CD (one per student).

 **Bible Lesson**

Scripture: Luke 15:1–7

INTRODUCING THE STORY

If Jesus were invited to a meal with hundreds of other guests, who do you think He would sit by at the table? It seems like Jesus would like to spend time with very good Christians. It seems like He would like to sit by pastors and missionaries and people who have been Christians for a long time.

It would seem that Jesus would like to eat with people who talked like Christians, looked like Christians, and acted like Christians. Then Jesus and the people with whom He was eating could talk about how good it is to be a Christian and how they wish everyone else in the world were Christians, too.

Who do you think Jesus would sit by? "Then drew near unto him all the publicans and sinners for to hear him" (Luke 15:1). Many of the people Jesus spent time with didn't look like Christians, because they weren't. Some of them were publicans—tax collectors who often collected much more money than the people owed. That made these publicans thieves. Some of the people Jesus sat by and spoke to were murderers. Some of them were liars. Some of them worshipped idols.

The people Jesus spent time with were the people who needed Him— the people who weren't yet saved from their sins. In fact, Jesus looked for sinners to sit by, talk to, and spend time with. Jesus looked for sinners in order to be kind to them and show them love. Jesus wanted to spend time with them so He could show them how to be saved from their sins. He wanted to give them freedom from their sins.

> **Luke 19:10**
>
> 10 *For the Son of man is come to seek and to save that which was lost.*

Jesus was so loving to sinners that they wanted to hear what He had to say. They knew He was different than most of the religious people they had ever seen. They could see Jesus had peace and joy they had never seen before. They had seen Jesus heal sick people and they had heard Jesus tell people their sins were forgiven. Many sinners came to Jesus because they wanted to hear the truth about how to be forgiven from their sins.

But there were some people who spent time with Jesus who didn't want to hear the truth from Him. They didn't listen to Jesus so they could learn the truth—they listened to Him so they could show people that He was wrong. These were religious teachers who didn't trust in Jesus as their Saviour. They taught the people that the way to go to Heaven was by following their rules.

These religious leaders had rules about everything. They had rules about how to wash your hands. They had rules about how far you could walk on church days. They had rules about what you could eat and how to cook it. They had rules about everything, and they were very proud of their rules. Some of these religious leaders were called scribes, and some were called Pharisees.

When Jesus taught the people that the way to have your sins forgiven and go to Heaven is not through keeping rules, but through trusting Jesus as your Saviour, the scribes and Pharisees became very angry. They didn't want the publicans and sinners to be able to go to Heaven. They didn't want people of other nationalities to be able to go to Heaven. They didn't want murderers, thieves, and idol worshipers to be able to go to Heaven.

The scribes and Pharisees also became jealous of Jesus. They wanted to be the teachers that everyone went to when they wanted to learn about God. They wanted to be the ones the people respected and looked up to. They didn't want the average or ordinary people following Jesus, and they didn't want sinners to be saved. "And the Pharisees and scribes murmured, saying, This man receiveth sinners, and eateth with them" (Luke 15:2).

Jesus answered the Pharisees with a story. As you listen to the story, think about yourselves. Think what it would be like if you were the shepherd in the story, and one of your sheep got lost.

THE STORY

1. A Shepherd with One Hundred Sheep

Flash Card 7.1

A shepherd owned one hundred very ordinary sheep. Just like all the other sheep in the whole world, these sheep needed their shepherd. They didn't know when it was time to go out to the pasture; they didn't know where to go for the best grass, and they didn't know where to find good, clean water. They didn't know how to protect themselves from wild animals and thieves, and they didn't know how to stay out of dangerous places. Everywhere they went, and in everything they did, these very ordinary sheep needed their shepherd to lead them.

Day after day the shepherd led his sheep. Early in the morning, just as the sun was rising, he opened the door of the sheepfold and led his sheep to drink the refreshing dew off the grass. It was important for the shepherd to lead them to the dew before the sun rose high overhead and dried it all away. Then the shepherd led the sheep to further pastures—up in the hills, or down in the valleys. Everywhere the shepherd went, his sheep followed. Finally, each evening, the shepherd led his sheep back to the safety of the sheepfold.

The shepherd knew each of his one hundred sheep, and he even knew each of their names.

John 10:3b, 14

3b *He calleth his own sheep by name, and leadeth them out.*

14 *I am the good shepherd, and know my sheep, and am known of mine.*

He would often count them to make sure none had wandered away. If you were to walk into the wilderness where this shepherd was tending his sheep, you might hear him counting—"One, two, three, four…ninety-five, ninety-six, ninety-seven, ninety-eight, ninety-nine, one hundred. Yes, they're all here." Then you might hear the shepherd whistle a merry tune or play a song on his harp.

2. A Sheep Is Lost

Flash Card 7.2

The day came, however, when the shepherd didn't count one hundred sheep—there were only ninety-nine. A sheep was missing, and the shepherd knew exactly which sheep it was! The shepherd's heart pounded as he thought of his sheep alone, without her shepherd. "I have to find my sheep," the shepherd thought, as he left his ninety-nine sheep together in the wilderness and went off in search of his one lost sheep.

3. The Shepherd Searches for the Lost Sheep

"That sheep," the shepherd thought, "could be anywhere. If a bear or lion should find her, she will have no one to defend her, and she will be torn into pieces. If a thief comes to steal her, she won't know enough to run away, and she will be stolen by someone who won't know her, love her, and take good care of her. I have raised her since she was born. I've led her to green pastures and to clear water. I have poured oil and medicine on her wounds when she was injured. I often pulled her away from danger with my shepherd's staff when she was just a little lamb. She needs me, and I have find her."

"My sheep may have wandered away from the good pasture, and she won't know how to find healthy grass on her own. She might drink polluted (dirty) water, and then she will get sick, with no one to give her medicine to make her well again. She might get caught in a thorn bush or fall off a cliff. She will never be able to find her way home on her own, and if I don't find her, she will be lost for good."

All the shepherd could think about was finding his sheep so he could bring her back to the safety of his care. The shepherd started into a run. "I have to find her before dark!"

The shepherd didn't think about the jagged rocks that were bruising his feet. He didn't think about the thorns that were tearing his robe and cutting his face and arms. He barely noticed the hot sun beating down on him. He just kept on—sometimes walking, sometimes running, and all the time calling for his sheep.

Now and then the shepherd would come upon another shepherd on some hill. "Have you seen a wandering sheep?" he would call across the field. Always the reply was the same, "No, I haven't seen her."

The shepherd kept on searching. He looked under every bush and jagged rock. He looked behind every tree. And as he looked, the shepherd listened carefully. He hoped to hear the bleating of his lost sheep. He knew his sheep would be tired by now, and the "baa" of his lost sheep might be very faint (quiet). The shepherd kept walking, running, looking, and listening.

4. The Shepherd Finds His Sheep

At last, the shepherd found his lost sheep! There she was, caught in a thorn bush, alone, hurt, and afraid. "Oh, here you are, little sheep," the kind

shepherd spoke gently as he poured oil on her wounds. "I've been looking all over for you—I just had to find you, you poor, poor sheep. Who would have taken care of you if I hadn't found you? Who would have known you and loved you? Who would have taken you to the best pasture and brought you to clean water? And I would have missed you desperately. You are my own dear sheep, and I am so glad to have you back with me!" Then, with a song of joy in his heart, the shepherd lifted his sheep off the ground and onto his shoulders, and he began the long, hard journey back to his ninety-nine sheep.

The journey back was dangerous, just as it was when the shepherd was searching for his lost sheep. But the shepherd didn't think about the jagged rocks and the thorny bushes. He didn't think about the lions and bears that may be waiting to attack. The shepherd whistled and sang as he carried his poor sheep back to the sheepfold. The shepherd's heart was full of joy over his sheep that wasn't lost anymore.

5. The Shepherd Rejoices with His Friends and Neighbors

When the shepherd arrived back home, he ran to all his friends and neighbors. "Look here!" he called. "My sheep that was lost is found! I searched all over the countryside for her. I was afraid she wouldn't have anyone to take care of her, and she would surely be torn in pieces by some lion or bear. I knew she could never find her way home by herself. But, here she is! I found her, caught in a thorny bush. I have carried her home, and I am so glad she is found! I know you are happy for me, too." The shepherd was so full of happiness that he almost skipped as he shared his joy with his friends. He barely noticed the weight of his sheep on his shoulders.

Teaching Tip

If you are physically able, skip and jump and twirl in circles as the shepherd finds his lost sheep.

JESUS EXPLAINS THE STORY

"Now, what if that were you?" Jesus asked the Pharisees and scribes. "Wouldn't you leave the ninety-nine sheep in order to find your lost sheep?"

"The story I just told," He went on to say, "was about Heaven. Just as there was joy over one sheep that was found, there is joy in Heaven over one sinner who turns away from his sin and turns to the Saviour, Jesus Christ" (from Luke 15:7).

Oh, the shepherd was glad to have his ninety-nine sheep that didn't get lost—he loved them just as much as he loved his lost sheep. But he knew the ninety-nine were safe under his care. So, for now, the shepherd rejoiced especially over the lost sheep that was now found.

People are like sheep. They are lost in their sin, and they need to be found. The Shepherd, the Lord Jesus Christ, suffered and paid the price for the sins of all the people in the whole world. Just as the shepherd went through pain and suffering in order to bring his lost sheep back home, Jesus suffered on the Cross to make a way for lost people to have our sins forgiven and live with Him in Heaven forever.

Isaiah 53:6

6 *All we like sheep have gone astray; we have turned every one to his own way; and the LORD hath laid on him the iniquity of us all.*

Jesus chose to be hurt in order to save us from our sins. He chose to die on the Cross and shed His blood so we could be saved from our sins. Jesus is the Good Shepherd we learned about last week. He loves us, and He wants us to be with Him forever.

Like sheep, people wander about. They don't know how to take care of themselves on their own. They didn't make themselves, so they don't know what is best for themselves. They have an enemy (Satan) who would like to destroy them and lead them away from the Shepherd.

1 Peter 5:8b

8b *Your adversary the devil, as a roaring lion, walketh about, seeking whom he may devour:*

Lost people, like lost sheep, need the Shepherd—Jesus—to search for them. And that is exactly what Jesus does.

Luke 19:10

10 *For the Son of man is come to seek and to save that which was lost.*

Teaching Tip

Luke 19:10 would be appropriate to use either here or in the introduction, as suggested. You may wish to use it both places.

Just like the sheep couldn't get home by herself, we can't get to Heaven by ourselves. We wander about, trying this and trying that, not knowing that it's really the Good Shepherd who will make us happiest of all. We need to trust the Good Shepherd as our Saviour from sin.

John 10:11

11   I am the good shepherd: the good shepherd giveth his life
for the sheep.

When a lost person is found by the Good Shepherd, the Shepherd carries him on His strong shoulders. The Good Shepherd is full of joy over the lost person who has been saved. Jesus said the angels in Heaven rejoice with God over one person who is saved, just as the shepherd's friends and neighbors rejoiced with him when he found his lost sheep.

Jesus said to the Pharisees and scribes, "You wonder why I spend time with sinful people? It's because they need me. They need to be found—they need to be saved from their sins. If they weren't lost in their sins, they wouldn't need a Saviour. I am the Saviour they need. And I am the Saviour you need, too."

"I still rejoice over the salvation of those who have already been forgiven of their sins—those who were already found. Now I seek other lost people so they too can trust the Good Shepherd as their Saviour from sin."

APPLYING THE STORY

This whole world is lost and needs to be found. Nobody goes to Heaven because they follow the rules of the scribes and Pharisees or even because they follow the rules of the Bible.

No one, except Jesus, ever has followed all the rules, or commandments, in the Bible. Everyone has sinned and needs to be forgiven by the Good Shepherd, Jesus Christ.

Romans 3:23

23   For all have sinned, and come short of the glory of God.

Jesus is the only one who can forgive sins. He paid for our sins with His own blood when He died on the Cross.

Have you asked the Good Shepherd to be your Saviour from sin? Have you realized that you were lost from Him and the only way you could be found is to ask Him to forgive you of your sins and be your Saviour?

He will do that today, if you ask Him. If you want to trust Jesus today as your Saviour from sin, ask one of the teachers after class, and we will be happy to lead you to the Good Shepherd who will forgive your sins and give you a home with Him in Heaven. When you are saved from your sin, Heaven will rejoice over you, too!

If you have already trusted Jesus as your Saviour, your Good Shepherd wants to lead you. He wants you to stay close by His side and never wander away from Him. He wants to protect you from attacks by the enemy (Satan). He keeps you safe as you read and follow His Word and as you trust Him.

Do you follow close by your Shepherd—the one who gave His life for you? What are some things you can do to stay close to Him?

- Talk to Him every day through prayer.
- Listen to Him through reading the Bible and listening to the messages in church and Sunday school.
- Obey His commands and directions.
- Introduce Him to others by sharing the Gospel with them.

He wants you to always stay close to Him by following, loving, and obeying Him. He is the very best Shepherd you can ever have. He is the Good Shepherd.

Finding the Lost Sheep

Materials Needed

Game pieces on the Ministry Resource CD

Instructions

Print and cut games pieces. Laminate for durability. Before students arrive hide the sheep cards around the room.

Divide the class into two teams. Ask Team 1 a review question. If the student answers correctly, allow him to look for a sheep. He can bring it to you and his team receives the points. Repeat with Team 2. The team with the most points wins.

1. What two groups of religious leaders were jealous of Jesus?
    Answer: The scribes and the Pharisees

2. What is the job of a shepherd?
    Answer: To lead and take care of his sheep

3. How many sheep did the shepherd in our story have?
    Answer: 100

4. This shepherd knew his sheep very well. Name one unique fact he knew about each of his sheep.
    Answer: He knew the names of each of his sheep.

5. What happened to one of the shepherd's sheep?
    Answer: One of the sheep got lost.

6. What did the shepherd do when one of the sheep went missing?
    Answer: The shepherd left the other ninety-nine sheep to find the one that was lost.

7. Did the shepherd find his lost sheep?
    Answer: Yes!

8. What did the shepherd do when he found his sheep?
    Answer: He rejoiced.

9. Just as the found sheep made the shepherd rejoice, what makes Heaven rejoice?

    Answer: Heaven rejoices when one sinner turns from his sin and turns to Jesus as Saviour.

10. What are some things you can do to stay close to your Shepherd?

    Answer: Answers will vary but may include examples given on page 108.

 # Teaching the Memory Verse

John 15:13

13   Greater love hath no man than this, that a man lay down his life for his friends.

Print the verse from the Ministry Resource CD on cardstock. Laminate for durability.

Have the students find John 15:13 in their Bibles. Read the verse together and explain that is what Jesus did for us. He laid down His life for us! He loves us that much. Jesus loves us with the greatest love.

Show the class the first flash card, and give them the correct wording of each picture. Then say this flash card together. Have a student come to the front and hold the flash card. Repeat with the rest of the flash cards.

Object Lesson—I Lost It!

Materials Needed:
A bag full of small stuffed toys

For the teacher:
Hide one of the toys ahead of time.

To the Class:
Many children make a hobby of collecting things. For example, they may collect coins, stamps, baseball cards, dolls, or miniature cars. Some may even collect items from nature like bugs, butterflies, or seashells! Have you ever collected anything?

I have a very nice collection of stuffed toys. They come in all shapes and sizes. Today I brought some of them to show to you. (Show the children the stuffed toys, commenting on each as you show it to them.)

Oh, my! I seem to have lost one of my stuffed toys. I know I had it when I got here this morning. Would you help me look for it? (Lead the children in a search for the lost toy. When it is found, continue the lesson.) Thank you so much for helping me find the lost toy. Even though I have a very large collection, every one of them is very important to me, and I would be very upset if one of them was lost.

Application:
Jesus never gives up on a lost sheep. Every single one of His children is very special to Him. Think about your collection of toys. What if one of your toys was missing? How would you feel?

Our toys are important to us, but on a much greater scale, we are important to Jesus! Read Luke 15:3–7.

Craft—Sheep

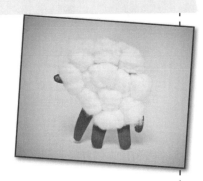

Getting It Together

Black cardstock or construction paper
Cotton balls
Scissors
Glue

Per Student:
1   verse template located on the Ministry Resource CD
1   craft eye

Putting It Together

1.   Print and cut out the Lesson 7 craft verse template from the Ministry Resource CD.
2.   Have each child trace their hand on black cardstock.
3.   Cut out the traced hand.
4.   Glue the craft eye to the thumb of the hand.
5.   Glue cotton balls on the hand, being careful not to glue any cotton balls to the traced fingers.
6.   Glue or tape the memory verse to the back of the hand.

Seeing It Together

Jesus is our Good Shepherd, and we are His sheep. We need to be thankful for such a wonderful Shepherd who loves us so much that He is willing to lay down His life for us!

Additional Resources

Find the following items on the Ministry Resource CD:

- Coloring Page (for younger children)
- Activity Page (for older children)
- Student Take-Home Paper
- PowerPoint Presentation

Suggested Classroom Schedule

Before Class	Complete attendance record. Provide students with coloring/activity pages.	
Opening	Welcome	
Prayer	Prayer requests and praise reports from the children	
Song Time		
Memory Verse	Psalm 40:8	
Song Time		
Object Lesson	Obedience First	
Bible Lesson	The Loving Father	
Application/Invitation	Help saved students apply lesson. Invite unsaved students to receive Christ.	
Snack	Heart-shaped Bread	
Review Game/Questions	Zonk	
Craft	Journal	
Closing	Give announcements and pray. Distribute take-home papers.	

Lesson Eight Overview

The Loving Father
Theme—Follow God's will.

Scripture
Luke 15:11–32

Memory Verse
Psalm 40:8—"*I delight to do thy will, O my God: yea, thy law is within my heart.*"

Lesson Outline

Introducing the Story
Today we will learn about an unhappy son who decided to go his own way. This son was unhappy because he forgot to be thankful for all the good things his father did for him. Let's look in our Bibles to see what happened to this son and his father.

Telling the Story
1. **The Father with Two Sons** (v. 11)
2. **An Unhappy Son** (v. 12)—*Flash Card 8.1*
3. **The Younger Son Leaves Home** (v. 13)
4. **A Famine in the Land** (v. 14), *Proverbs 23:5*
5. **The Younger Son Finds a Job** (vv. 15–19)—*Flash Card 8.2*
6. **The Younger Son Returns Home** (vv. 20–21)
7. **The Father Celebrates** (vv. 22–24)—*Flash Card 8.3*
8. **The Older Brother** (vv. 25–30)
9. **The Father's Explanation** (vv. 31–32)

Applying the Story (*Galatians 6:7*)
God is like the father in the parable of the Prodigal Son. He is very sad when you sin. You can choose to follow God and to have the blessings that come through obedience.

8 Lesson Eight

The Loving Father

Theme: Follow God's will.

Scripture

Luke 15:11–32

11 And he said, A certain man had two sons:

12 And the younger of them said to his father, Father, give me the portion of goods that falleth to me. And he divided unto them his living.

13 And not many days after the younger son gathered all together, and took his journey into a far country, and there wasted his substance with riotous living.

14 And when he had spent all, there arose a mighty famine in that land; and he began to be in want.

15 And he went and joined himself to a citizen of that country; and he sent him into his fields to feed swine.

16 And he would fain have filled his belly with the husks that the swine did eat: and no man gave unto him.

17 And when he came to himself, he said, How many hired servants of my father's have bread enough and to spare, and I perish with hunger!

18 I will arise and go to my father, and will say unto him, Father, I have sinned against heaven, and before thee,

19 And am no more worthy to be called thy son: make me as one of thy hired servants.

20 And he arose, and came to his father. But when he was yet a great way off, his father saw him, and had compassion, and ran, and fell on his neck, and kissed him.

21 And the son said unto him, Father, I have sinned against heaven, and in thy sight, and am no more worthy to be called thy son.

22 But the father said to his servants, Bring forth the best robe, and put it on him; and put a ring on his hand, and shoes on his feet:

23 And bring hither the fatted calf, and kill it; and let us eat, and be merry:

Memory Verse

Psalm 40:8
"I delight to do thy will, O my God: yea, thy law is within my heart."

24   *For this my son was dead, and is alive again; he was lost, and is found. And they began to be merry.*

25   *Now his elder son was in the field: and as he came and drew nigh to the house, he heard musick and dancing.*

26   *And he called one of the servants, and asked what these things meant.*

27   *And he said unto him, Thy brother is come; and thy father hath killed the fatted calf, because he hath received him safe and sound.*

28   *And he was angry, and would not go in: therefore came his father out, and intreated him.*

29   *And he answering said to his father, Lo, these many years do I serve thee, neither transgressed I at any time thy commandment: and yet thou never gavest me a kid, that I might make merry with my friends:*

30   *But as soon as this thy son was come, which hath devoured thy living with harlots, thou hast killed for him the fatted calf.*

31   *And he said unto him, Son, thou art ever with me, and all that I have is thine.*

32   *It was meet that we should make merry, and be glad: for this thy brother was dead, and is alive again; and was lost, and is found.*

Teacher's Checklist

- ❑ Read Luke 15:11–32 daily.
- ❑ Study Lesson 8.
- ❑ Flash cards 8.1–8.3
- ❑ Prepare snack—heart-shaped bread.
- ❑ Gather for lesson—bucket.
- ❑ Gather for review game—envelopes.
- ❑ Print and cut out "Zonk" game pieces from the Ministry Resource CD.
- ❑ Print verse flash cards from the Ministry Resource CD.
- ❑ Gather for object lesson—musical instruments, noise makers, party horns, pots or pans.
- ❑ Purchase for craft—foam craft letters and stickers.
- ❑ Print for craft—template from the Ministry Resource CD (1 per student).
- ❑ Gather for craft—white paper, stapler, 1 piece of colored cardstock per student.
- ❑ Print and duplicate Coloring Pages or Activity Pages on the Ministry Resource CD (one per student).
- ❑ Print and duplicate Take Home Paper on the Ministry Resource CD (one per student).

 ## Snack Suggestion

Serve the students heart-shaped bread. Use a heart cookie cutter to cut heart shapes out of refrigerator bread dough. Cook according to package directions. Encourage the children to follow God from their hearts.

Bible Lesson

Scripture: Luke 15:11–32

INTRODUCING THE STORY

Have you ever wondered what it would be like to have as much money as you wanted? It's fun to think of all the things you would buy. Maybe you would buy a new home for your parents or grandparents. Maybe you would buy a new car for your family. Maybe you would buy games or a swimming pool. Maybe you would give a million dollars to a missionary.

Jesus told a story about a young man who did have as much money as he wanted, but he didn't use his money for the right things. In fact, he didn't want to use his money for the right things, and he had to pay a very high price for his wrong choices.

This story is called "The Prodigal Son."

THE STORY

1. A Father with Two Sons (v. 11)

A hard-working man had two sons. This father loved each of his sons with all his heart. He was a good father—he loved his two sons the same.

Each day as the father worked in his fields, he thought of his two sons, and how one day they would own everything he had. "It's a joy to work hard so my boys can have a good inheritance after I am gone," the father said to himself as he plowed and raked and hoed. The father earned a lot of money—his sons would have a large inheritance.

Work and money were not the most important things to this father. He loved God, and he wanted his sons to love God too. He taught his sons about God and about salvation, and he taught them how God wanted them to live. He prayed many times a day for his sons. Every morning and evening he prayed with his sons because he wanted his sons to learn how to pray.

The father's sons were more important to him than anything in the world. They were more important to him than money. They were more important than his job. They were more important than his house, barns, and fields. They were more important than friends, sports, and hobbies.

Teaching Tip

Ask your students what they would buy if they had a lot of money. This will give you insight into their values and may provide you with future gift ideas, as well.

Teacher's Note

Prodigal:
"one who is wasteful or extravagant; a reckless spendthrift"

Teacher's Note

Inheritance:
"property or possessions received after a parent or guardian dies"

More than anything else, the father wanted his sons to have happy lives serving God, and he taught them how to do just that.

2. An Unhappy Son (v. 12)

A problem came into the younger son's life. He forgot to be thankful for all the good things his father did for him and for all the good things his father gave him. He forgot to be thankful to God for the good father He had given him. He stopped reading his Bible and he stopped praying.

The younger son started spending time with young men who didn't love the Lord—friends who lied and cheated and didn't honor their parents. The son wasn't happy living with his father anymore. One day, the younger son made a request that made his father very sad.

"And the younger of them said to his father, Father, give me the portion of goods that falleth to me…" (Luke 15:12a).

Flash Card 8.1

"What?" the father thought. "Why does my son want his inheritance now—while I am still alive? What has happened to my son? What will he do with all this money? He isn't old enough and wise enough to spend it on things that will last. He hasn't been walking with God, and this money will likely get him into trouble that will damage or destroy his life. I love my son so much, and I am sorry to see him make foolish decisions—I just wish he could see how he is hurting himself."

"But, the money is his," the father said sadly to himself. "He will have it sooner or later, and he wants it now. I can't make him stay, and I can't make him do right. I will give it to him."

"And he divided unto them his living" (Luke 15:12b). With a broken heart, the father divided the inheritance between his two sons.

3. The Younger Son Leaves Home (v. 13)

"And not many days after the younger son gathered all together, and took his journey into a far country, and there wasted his substance with riotous living" (Luke 15:13).

The younger son went as far away from his father's home as he could go. He didn't want to think about his father. He didn't want to think about

Teacher's Note

Riotous:
"disorderly; without restraint; excessive in expensive indulgences, such as eating, drinking, or other sensual pleasures"

what his father had taught him from the time he was born. He just wanted to have a good time, and he had plenty of money to do it.

So, the younger son began living just like he wanted to. He didn't have rules anymore. He could do whatever he wanted. He could choose his own friends. He could buy whatever he wanted to buy, for he had plenty of money now. He had half his father's money, and now he could enjoy life, he thought.

If the younger son saw something he wanted, he bought it. He didn't care how much it cost, because he had a large sum of money—enough to last for a long, long time, he thought. If he saw someone he wanted to be friends with, he invited them to go out with him, and he spent money to buy things for them. He bought all the food and drink and fun you could imagine. And he never even thought about his father.

4. A Famine in the Land (v. 14)

The day came, however, when the younger son had spent all the money his father had given him. He couldn't believe it—his money was all gone! Where did it all go? He had thought it would last forever!

Teacher's Note

Famine:
"extreme scarcity or lack of food"

Proverbs 23:5

5   *Wilt thou set thine eyes upon that which is not? for riches certainly make themselves wings; they fly away as an eagle toward heaven.*

Now the younger son had no home, no money, and no food. He would need to find a job.

Something happened in the land that the younger son didn't expect. "There arose a mighty famine in that land" (Luke 15:14). Now no one in the land had enough food. No one would be able to hire the younger son to work for them, because no one had enough money to pay him.

What would he do now? Here he was, all alone in a strange land—no home, no food, no money—and a famine!

The younger son walked around the city, going from one business to another, asking for work; but no one had money to pay him. The younger son went out into the countryside. He went to one farm after another, asking for work. No one would hire him on the farms, either.

5. The Younger Son Finds a Job (vv. 15–19)

Finally, the last farmer, down at the end of the long road gave the younger son a job. The farmer said, "I need someone to feed my pigs. You think you can feed pigs, boy?"

The younger son hung his head, nodded, and started off to the field, carrying a bucket of pig feed.

Out in the field with the pigs, the younger son noticed a terrible, empty feeling deep in his stomach. He realized how very hungry he had become. "Why, I haven't eaten for days!" he thought to himself. "Look at all the food these pigs get. You know, it actually doesn't look that bad. Maybe I'll just have a little…."

The younger son shook himself. "What am I doing? What was I thinking? How many hired servants of my father's have bread enough and to spare, and I perish with hunger! I will arise and go to my father, and will say unto him, Father, I have sinned against heaven, and before thee, And am no more worthy to be called thy son: make me as one of thy hired servants" (Luke 15:17–19). "Yes, I'll go home and ask my father to forgive me. I'll ask him to hire me, just like a servant. My father's servants don't have to eat pig's food—they have everything they need."

Act It Out

Feed the Pigs
Use a bucket, preferably an old-looking one, as the son goes out to feed the swine. Act it out as the prodigal son comes close to eating the pigs' food.

Flash Card 8.2

6. The Younger Son Returns Home (vv. 20–21)

"And he arose, and came to his father. But when he was yet a great way off, his father saw him, and had compassion, and ran, and fell on his neck, and kissed him" (Luke 15:20). His father saw him while he was still far away. His father had been waiting for him! His father had been watching for him! His father wasn't angry with him! His father had compassion on his son and ran to him and hugged him and kissed him.

"And the son said unto him, Father, I have sinned against heaven, and in thy sight, and am no more worthy to be called thy son" (Luke 15:21). The son said just what he had planned to say when he was in the field with the pigs. He told his father he was sorry and that he didn't deserve to be his son anymore.

7. The Father Celebrates (vv. 22–24)

Flash Card 8.3

But the father called his servants. "Bring the best robe, and put it on my son. Bring also a ring for his finger, and shoes for his feet. Prepare a feast—make a party for my son. It was like my son was dead, and he's alive again. He was lost, and now he's found. Oh, this is reason to celebrate!"

He turned to his son and said, "Why, you are my own son! I'm not going to give you a job as a servant! You are my son, just as you've always been. I am so glad you are back home!"

And there was a great party for the younger son who had finally come home.

8. The Older Brother (vv. 25–30)

While everyone in the house was celebrating, the older son was still at work in the field. As he walked home in the evening, he began to hear music and celebrating. "And he called one of the servants, and asked what these things meant" (Luke 15:26).

"Why, haven't you heard?" asked the servant. "It's your younger brother—he's come home! Your father is so happy. He has made a great party to celebrate your younger brother's return. Come join us."

The older brother didn't feel like celebrating. In fact, the older brother felt angry in his heart. "I won't go in and celebrate with them. Why would they celebrate when my younger brother has wasted everything my father gave him?"

The father came out to his older son. "Son, why aren't you joining us for the party? Your brother is home, and he wants to see you."

"I have always obeyed and served you, Father," said the older brother angrily. "I never disobeyed any command you gave. And you have never invited my friends over for a party. You have never had a feast in my honor. But your younger son, who has wasted all your money—as soon as he comes home, you make a party for him! It's just not fair!"

9. The Father's Explanation (vv. 31–32)

"Son," the father said, "you have been with me all these years. I'm so thankful for you and for your obedience. Your younger brother has, as you said,

The Stories of Our Saviour | © 2011 Striving Together Publications

wasted all his inheritance. Everything I have left is yours, and it will continue to be yours. Yes, you have been a faithful son.

"But your brother—he went off into a far country. He went down the wrong road. He made the wrong choices. He wasted his money, and he wasted part of his life. It was like he was lost, but now he's found. It was like he was dead, but now he's alive.

"Your brother is sorry, now. He's learned his lesson. He wishes he hadn't done what he did. It's time for us to celebrate now, because your brother is back with us, and his heart is right with his father, and, most importantly of all, with his Lord."

APPLYING THE STORY

The younger son in Jesus' story (he was the prodigal son) thought he was missing out on things that would make him happy. He grew tired of obeying his father's rules. He grew tired of serving his father. He grew tired of following the Bible.

So, he went his own way. He demanded his inheritance from his father, left home, and bought himself everything he had ever wanted. But the younger son (the prodigal) didn't think about the future. He didn't think what would happen to him if he lived in disobedience to his father and disobedience to God.

Have you ever felt like the younger son did before he left home? Have you ever thought it was hard to keep God's rules and your parents' rules, and that life would just be easier if you did what you wanted to?

That's the way it is any time you sin. You may not be able to leave home with half of your father's money, but you still go your own way:

- When you don't do something your parents told you to do
- When you do something your parents told you not to do
- When you lie
- When you cheat at school
- When you call names or hit a friend or brother or sister
- When you say bad words
- When you take something that isn't yours

Teaching Tip

Add to this list of sins what is appropriate for your age group and specific students in your class.

Satan is our enemy who tempts us to feel like living for the Lord is hard. He tries to take our minds away from the peace and joy that God wants to give us when we obey Him. He tries to take our minds away from our

Heavenly Father's great love for us. He tries to take our minds away from the fact that there is always a penalty for sin.

Galatians 6:7

7　*Be not deceived; God is not mocked: for whatsoever a man soweth, that shall he also reap.*

The younger son paid a great price for going his own way.

- He lost his money.
- He lost his friends.
- He didn't have a home, food, bed, or warm clothes.
- He found himself so hungry that he wanted to eat pigs' food.
- He didn't have his father's advice and wisdom to help him make decisions.
- He couldn't feel the love of his father.

When you are tempted to go your own way, remember who it is who is tempting you—your enemy. Any time you disobey your parents or the Bible, you are going your own way, and you miss out on the good things God wants to give you. Some wrong decisions you make while you are young will damage your whole life, even though they seem to be very small decisions. Just as the younger son didn't choose the price he paid for his sin, you can't choose what will happen in your life as a result of your sin. But you can choose to follow God and to have the blessings that come through obedience.

God is like the father in the parable of the Prodigal Son. He is grieved (very disappointed and saddened) when you sin, just as the younger son's father was when his son chose to go away.

And, just like the father in the parable, God has compassion on you. When you go your own way (that's sin) your Heavenly Father lovingly waits for you to go to Him. When you go to Him, telling Him you have sinned, He rejoices, just as the father did in the story. He is not angry with you. He is waiting for you. He is waiting to celebrate. He is waiting to help you live for Him again.

As I pray, ask God to show you in your heart ways you have gone your own way. Ask Him to show you sins that you have committed that you have not asked Him to forgive you for. Then, when He reminds you, ask Him to

　　　　The Stories of Our Saviour | © 2011 Striving Together Publications

forgive you. He is waiting for you to go to Him. He is waiting to forgive you and for you to live for Him again.

Your Heavenly Father wants you to go home to Him, just as the prodigal son went home to his father. Your Father will never leave you. And He wants you to always stay close to Him as well.

 ## Review Game/Questions

Zonk
Materials Needed
- Game pieces for "Zonk" found on the Ministry Resource CD.
- Envelopes

Instructions
Print and cut games pieces. Laminate for durability. Place one game piece in each envelope. Keep the envelopes in sets of three. There should be one high point card, one low point card and one "Zonk" for each set. Number the envelopes "1," "2," and "3." Rotate the cards that go in the envelopes, for example not all number three envelopes should contain "Zonk."

Divide the class into two teams. When a student answers a review question correctly, show him a set of three envelopes. Allow the student to pick one. Open the envelope. If the card contains points, award them to the team. If the card is a "Zonk," no points are given.

1. How many sons did the father in our story have?
   Answer: Two

2. What did the younger, unhappy son tell his father to give him?
   Answer: His inheritance

3. What did the younger son do once his father gave him his inheritance?
   Answer: He gathered his stuff and left for a far country.

4. How did the younger son spend his inheritance?
   Answer: He wasted it on riotous living.

5. What happened in the land where the younger son lived?
   Answer: There was a famine—a lack of food.

6. What was the prodigal son's job?
   Answer: He fed pigs

7. How did the father respond when his prodigal son returned home?
   Answer: He ran to him and embraced him. He celebrated by bringing out the best clothing. He prepared a great feast.

8. How did the older brother respond when the prodigal son returned?
   Answer: He was angry.

9. Why did the father celebrate his prodigal son's return?
   Answer: The father loved the son no matter what he did.

10. How does Jesus feel toward you when you've done wrong?
    Answer: He has compassion. He lovingly waits for us to return to him and ask for his forgiveness.

Teaching the Memory Verse

Psalm 40:8

8   *I delight to do thy will, O my God: yea, thy law is within my heart.*

Print flash cards and laminate for durability. Place flash cards on the chalkboard tray. Have the students find Psalm 40:8 in their Bibles.

When Mom and Dad give us a chore to do, how do they want us to respond? Usually they want us to have good attitudes, smiles on our faces, joy in our hearts. God wants us to do His will with a good attitude as well. Delighting to do what God wants us to do is a choice for us. Let's choose wisely.

Have the class read the verse together emphasizing the first word, and read the second time emphasizing the second word. Continue this pattern throughout the verse. For example:

I delight to do thy will, O my God: yea, thy law is within my heart.
I **delight** to do thy will, O my God: yea, thy law is within my heart.
I delight **to** do thy will, O my God: yea, thy law is within my heart.
I delight to **do** thy will, O my God: yea, thy law is within my heart.
I delight to do **thy** will, O my God: yea, thy law is within my heart.
I delight to do thy **will**, O my God: yea, thy law is within my heart.
I delight to do thy will, **O** my God: yea, thy law is within my heart.
I delight to do thy will, O **my** God: yea, thy law is within my heart.
I delight to do thy will, O my **God**: yea, thy law is within my heart.
I delight to do thy will, O my God: **yea**, thy law is within my heart.
I delight to do thy will, O my God: yea, **thy** law is within my heart.
I delight to do thy will, O my God: yea, thy **law** is within my heart.
I delight to do thy will, O my God: yea, thy law **is** within my heart.
I delight to do thy will, O my God: yea, thy law is **within** my heart.
I delight to do thy will, O my God: yea, thy law is within **my** heart.
I delight to do thy will, O my God: yea, thy law is within my **heart**.

Object Lesson—Obedience First

Materials Needed:
Musical instruments, noise makers, party horns, pots or pans—anything that makes noise

Lesson:
Pass out these items before you begin to explain the lesson. Explain to the children that you are handing these out to them and you only want them to play them when you ask them to. Explain that this is a matter of obedience. Review the story of the Prodigal Son and have them play the instruments when it was time to celebrate. The father had a huge party when the son returned home. The father wasn't mad at his son but accepted him the way he was.

Application:
That is exactly how Jesus is with His children. Jesus wants to have a personal relationship with us. When we go to Him, cofessing our sin and committing to follow Him, He rejoices! He welcomes us with open arms, because He loves us.

Additional Resources

Find the following items on the Ministry Resource CD:

- Coloring Page (for younger children)
- Activity Page (for older children)
- Student Take-Home Paper
- PowerPoint Presentation

Getting It Together

Foam craft letters
Foam craft stickers
White paper
Stapler

Per student:

1   craft template from the Ministry
    Resource CD
1   piece of colored cardstock

Putting It Together

1.   Print the Lesson 8 craft template out on white paper.
2.   Fold the white paper in half.
3.   Fold the piece of cardstock in half for the cover of the journal.
4.   Have each child decorate the journal.
5.   Open the cover and put the white paper in it.
6.   Staple the pages together to form a book. (Another option would be to hole punch the edge of the book and tie it together with ribbon.)

Seeing It Together

Jesus is our loving Heavenly Father, and He wants us to do His will throughout our lives. One important way to know and do God's will is through prayer. You can use this journal to help you thank your Heavenly Father and bring any requests to Him. It will be exciting to see how Jesus will guide you in His will as you faithfully pray to Him.

Suggested Classroom Schedule

Before Class	Complete attendance record. Provide students with coloring/activity pages.
Opening	Welcome
Prayer	Prayer requests and praise reports from the children
Song Time	
Memory Verse	Ephesians 2:8–9
Song Time	
Object Lesson	Going to Heaven!
Bible Lesson	The Rich Man and Lazarus
Application/Invitation	Help saved students apply lesson. Invite unsaved students to receive Christ.
Snack	Finger sandwiches and water
Review Game/Questions	Correct or Consequences
Craft	Invitation
Closing	Give announcements and pray. Distribute take-home papers.

Lesson Nine Overview

The Rich Man and Lazarus

Theme—We are saved by grace.

Scripture
Luke 16:19–31

Memory Verses
Ephesians 2:8–9—*"For by grace are ye saved through faith; and that not of yourselves: it is the gift of God: Not of works, lest any man should boast."*

Lesson Outline

Introducing the Story
Today's story is about a beggar and a very rich man. Jesus tells us that their lives end in a very surprising way! Let's look into our Bibles and find out what happens.

Telling the Story
1. The Rich Man (v. 19)— *Flash Card 9.1*
2. The Poor Man—Lazarus (vv. 20–21)— *Flash Card 9.2*
3. The Poor Man Dies (v.22) — *Flash Card 9.3*
4. The Rich Man Dies (v. 22)
5. The Rich Man Cries for Mercy (vv.23–24, *Genesis 15:6*)
6. Abraham Answers the Rich Man (vv.25–26)
7. The Rich Man Makes a Second Request (vv.27–28)
8. Abraham Answers Again (v. 29, *Romans 10:17*)
9. The Rich Man's Final Plea (v. 30)
10. Abraham's Final Answer (v. 31)

Applying the Story (*Ephesians 2:8–9, Romans 6:23a*)
Jesus says that it is only by grace that we will be saved from our sin and go to Heaven. Grace is God giving us something good that we don't deserve. Have you accepted God's grace?

9 Lesson Nine

The Rich Man and Lazarus

Theme: We are saved by grace.

 ## Scripture

Luke 16:19–31

19　There was a certain rich man, which was clothed in purple and fine linen, and fared sumptuously every day:

20　And there was a certain beggar named Lazarus, which was laid at his gate, full of sores,

21　And desiring to be fed with the crumbs which fell from the rich man's table: moreover the dogs came and licked his sores.

22　And it came to pass, that the beggar died, and was carried by the angels into Abraham's bosom: the rich man also died, and was buried;

23　And in hell he lift up his eyes, being in torments, and seeth Abraham afar off, and Lazarus in his bosom.

24　And he cried and said, Father Abraham, have mercy on me, and send Lazarus, that he may dip the tip of his finger in water, and cool my tongue; for I am tormented in this flame.

25　But Abraham said, Son, remember that thou in thy lifetime receivedst thy good things, and likewise Lazarus evil things: but now he is comforted, and thou art tormented.

26　And beside all this, between us and you there is a great gulf fixed: so that they which would pass from hence to you cannot; neither can they pass to us, that would come from thence.

27　Then he said, I pray thee therefore, father, that thou wouldest send him to my father's house:

28　For I have five brethren; that he may testify unto them, lest they also come into this place of torment.

29　Abraham saith unto him, They have Moses and the prophets; let them hear them.

30　And he said, Nay, father Abraham: but if one went unto them from the dead, they will repent.

Memory Verses

Ephesians 2:8–9
"For by grace are ye saved through faith; and that not of yourselves: it is the gift of God: Not of works, lest any man should boast."

31 *And he said unto him, If they hear not Moses and the prophets, neither will they be persuaded, though one rose from the dead.*

Snack Suggestion

Consider serving finger sandwiches and ice cold water. The rich man was tormented and asked God to let Lazarus dip his finger in water to cool his tongue. As the children eat the finger sandwiches and drink the cool water, ask them who they know who needs to hear about Jesus.

✔ Teacher's Checklist

- ❑ Read Luke 16:19–31 daily.
- ❑ Study Lesson 9.
- ❑ Flash cards 9.1–9.3
- ❑ Gather for lesson—old bathrobe and cup for beggar, can of peas, and Gospel tracts.
- ❑ Prepare snack—finger sandwiches and water.
- ❑ Print and cut out cards for review game from the Ministry Resource CD.
- ❑ Print memory verse (Ephesians 2:8–9) from the Visual Resource Packet.
- ❑ Gather for object lesson—balloons, paper plate, salt, and pepper.
- ❑ Gather for craft—ribbon, hole punch, colored paper, 1 tract per student, 1 clear bag per student.
- ❑ Print craft template for each student from the Ministry Resource CD.
- ❑ Print and duplicate Coloring Pages or Activity Pages on the Ministry Resource CD (one per student).
- ❑ Print and duplicate Take-Home Paper on the Ministry Resource CD (one per student).

Bible Lesson

Scripture: Luke 16:19–31

INTRODUCING THE STORY

Have you ever seen a beggar? A beggar is a person who can't provide for himself. He has no way to earn money, and he has to ask other people to give him money in order to be able to buy the things he needs just to live.

When Jesus walked on earth there were many beggars. Some of them were blind, and no one would hire them. Some of them couldn't work, and they had no way to get to a job, and no way to work. Some of them had other sicknesses that prevented them from being able to provide a living for themselves and their families. They had only rags for clothes, and they would hold out a cup, asking for money and food.

One day, Jesus told a story about a beggar, and how this beggar's life ended in a very surprising way!

Teaching Tip

Before class, dress up as a beggar. Wear an old, ragged bathrobe or sheet over your clothing. Smear a little chocolate or dark make-up on your face to make it look dirty. Bring an old cup to hold out as you ask for alms.

THE STORY

1. The Rich Man (v. 19)

"There was a certain rich man, which was clothed in purple and fine linen" (Luke 16:19). The rich man dressed like a king. Every night, before he went to bed, he called one of his servants. "Prepare my clothing for tomorrow. Make sure everything is perfect. I will wear my purple jacket and my finest linen shirt. Make sure my shirt is ironed, with not a wrinkle in it, and that there are no loose buttons. Polish my best shoes until they shine." After all, the rich man wanted everyone who saw him to know he was very important and very rich.

Not only did the rich man have beautiful, elegant clothes, but he ate fancy food every single day. Never did the rich man eat hot dogs, macaroni and cheese, or tacos for lunch. Cheerios and Rice Krispies were never seen on the rich man's breakfast table.

The rich man ate steak, lobster, and shrimp; and his desserts were the fanciest you could imagine! His butler served his food on the finest silver dishes. There were fresh flowers and elegant candles on his table for every

Flash Card 9.1

Teacher's Note

Butler:
"a manservant in charge of the dining room; usually the head servant in a household"

meal, and there was a new tablecloth every day. Yes, the rich man lived very elegantly—surely he had everything a man could wish for.

2. The Poor Man—Lazarus (vv. 20–21)

Flash Card 9.2

Teacher's Note

Alms:
"a gift or gifts for the poor"

Some people who lived near the rich man didn't have such fine lives. One man, in particular, was a beggar named Lazarus. Lazarus didn't have fancy clothes and he didn't have delicious food—Lazarus didn't have any food. Lazarus was so sick he couldn't walk, and he didn't have the strength to work. His body was covered with sores.

Every day, some kind person would carry Lazarus to the rich man's gate, where he would beg for alms. There he would lie, hoping the servants would give him scraps of leftover food from the rich man's table. "Just a few crumbs of food would calm this awful ache in my stomach," he would think weakly to himself.

Lazarus was hungry, and he was often cold. His were not fine clothes like the rich man's—Lazarus had only a few rags with which to cover himself.

Oh, Lazarus didn't lie alone at the rich man's gate. There were others who joined him. These others were hungry too, hoping for crumbs from the rich man's table. These others were dogs, and, as dogs will, they would lick the sores that covered Lazarus' body. Lazarus' life was very hard, indeed.

3. The Poor Man Dies (v. 22)

Flash Card 9.3

After some time, Lazarus died. There was no funeral for Lazarus. There were no relatives to cry and say how they missed him. There were no funeral flowers and no hymns played. In fact, hardly anyone at all noticed that Lazarus even had died.

There was One who knew, though. Lazarus had trusted the Lord Jesus Christ as his Saviour from sin, and now Lazarus was in Heaven with God. Lazarus would be with Jesus for ever and ever and ever.

Yes, Lazarus' life on earth had been hard. Yes, he had been sick. Yes, he had been poor. But now—now everything was perfect. He didn't even think about what life had been like for him. Now, he had no sores. Now, he had no pain. Now, he wasn't hungry. He was in Heaven, and now life was wonderful!

4. The Rich Man Dies (v. 22)

Sometime after Lazarus died, the rich man also died, and there was a magnificent funeral for him. His servants dressed him in his finest clothes, and his body was placed in a golden casket. Friends, neighbors, and relatives came from near and far, bringing flowers to decorate his grave. Singers sang beautiful songs as musicians played instruments. All the people at the funeral wept because the rich man was gone.

The rich man's life had been easy. Yes, he had owned everything his heart wished for. Yes, he had been strong and healthy. Yes, he had worn the finest clothes and eaten the finest food. Yes, he had always been warm and comfortable. But now—now everything had changed.

The rich man didn't go to Heaven. The rich man had never trusted the Lord Jesus Christ as his Saviour from sin, and now he was in the place the Bible calls Hell.

Now, the rich man had no fine clothes. Now, the rich man had no servants to take care of him. Now the rich man was alone. Now, the rich man was hungry. Now, the flames of Hell made the rich man always thirsty.

5. The Rich Man Cries for Mercy (vv. 23–24)

The rich man looked up, and far away he saw Lazarus, and he saw someone else as well. The rich man saw Abraham—another rich man who had lived many years earlier. Abraham was the great, great, great, great…grandfather of the whole nation of Israel. He was the very first Israelite, and the rich man was an Israelite. He just knew Abraham, his ancestor, would help him!

There was one difference, though, between the rich man Abraham, and the rich man in Hell. Abraham had trusted Jesus Christ as his Saviour, and the other rich man hadn't. That's why Abraham was in Heaven and this rich man was in Hell.

Genesis 15:6

6 *And he believed in the LORD; and he counted it to him for righteousness.*

The rich man cried out, "Father Abraham, have mercy on me, and send Lazarus, that he may dip the tip of his finger in water, and cool my tongue; for I am tormented in this flame" (Luke 16:24). "Please, send Lazarus with

Teacher's Note

Mercy:
"pity; compassion manifested toward a person in distress; kind or compassionate treatment of an offender, adversary, prisoner, etc. in one's power"

Teacher's Note

Tormented:
"put to extreme pain or anguish—the utmost degree of misery either of body or mind"

just a drop of water on his finger to cool my tongue. I am so miserable. Please, please, send Lazarus."

6. Abraham Answers the Rich Man (vv. 25–26)

Abraham called back to the rich man. "Son, remember that when you were living on earth your life was easy. You had every comfort of the world. You had good food every day, a soft bed, fine clothes, and servants. But you didn't trust Jesus. You thought only of yourself and living to please yourself. You didn't love God, and you didn't love other people.

"But remember Lazarus' life on earth—his life was hard. He was sick and covered with sores. He never had enough food and clothes, and he didn't have a soft bed to sleep on. He lay at your gate, wishing for you to give him a few crumbs.

"But Lazarus did love God. He did trust Jesus as his Saviour from sin. And now Lazarus is in Heaven, with only good and perfect things, and you are in the flames of Hell. And that's the way it will be forever and ever.

"Not only that, but no one in Heaven can pass over to Hell, and no one in Hell can pass to us in Heaven. Lazarus will always be in Heaven, and you will always be in Hell."

7. The Rich Man Makes a Second Request (vv. 27–28)

Then the rich man said, "Abraham, will you send Lazarus to my father's house? You see, I have five brothers who are just like I was. They live for pleasure, just like I did. They haven't trusted Jesus as their Saviour, either.

"I don't want my brothers to end up in Hell, like I am. If you send Lazarus, he can tell them how to be saved from their sins. I know they'll listen to him."

8. Abraham Answers Again (v. 29)

Abraham answered the rich man: "Your brothers have the Bible. They have preachers who have taught them the way of salvation. They can listen to them."

Romans 10:17

17   *So then faith cometh by hearing, and hearing by the word of God.*

9. The Rich Man's Final Plea (v. 30)

The rich man said, "Oh, Abraham, don't you know that if someone went to them from the dead and preached to them, then they would listen? They have had the Scriptures all their lives. They haven't believed them. They have heard preachers all their lives. They haven't listened to them. They would listen to someone who came back from the dead—I just know they would!"

10. Abraham's Final Answer (v. 31)

"If they don't believe the Bible," Abraham said, "they won't believe someone who rose from the dead. If they don't listen to the preachers, they won't listen to someone who rose from the dead."

APPLYING THE STORY

Did you notice how the roles reversed (changed) in the story?

- On earth, the rich man had every comfort he could wish for, while Lazarus was poor and needy.
- In Heaven, Lazarus had more comforts than the rich man had ever dreamed of: while in Hell, the rich man was poor and needy.
- On earth, Lazarus was in pain and the rich man was healthy.
- In Heaven, Lazarus was healed, while in Hell, the rich man was in terrible pain.
- On earth, Lazarus was a beggar.
- In Hell, the rich man was the beggar.

The rich man's life on earth was easy and comfortable. He never thought much about anyone else. He really didn't notice how miserable Lazarus was, lying at his very own gate. The rich man didn't think much about God, either.

Oh sure, the rich man knew about God. In fact, he believed in God. He even went to church sometimes. But the rich man never trusted in Jesus as his Saviour. The rich man really didn't believe that his money couldn't make him happy forever. He really didn't believe that if he didn't trust Jesus as his Saviour he would go to Hell when he died. He thought life would always be good for him, as it always had been.

Even with all the rich man's money, he could never purchase happiness forever. The time came when he died, and he wasn't prepared. He went to the place the Bible calls Hell, and he would be there, in pain and torment, forever.

Lazarus, on the other hand, didn't have an easy and comfortable life on earth. But Lazarus didn't spend his time thinking about how hard life was. Lazarus trusted Jesus as his Saviour from sin, and every day Lazarus thought about Heaven. Every day he wondered if this would be the day he would go to be with his Lord forever. Lazarus looked forward to Heaven.

There is no other way to go to Heaven than the way Lazarus chose. Some people believe they will go to Heaven because they give a lot of money to the church. Some people believe they will go to Heaven because they do good things for other people. Some people think they will go to Heaven because they take communion or because they were baptized. God's Word tells us that none of these things will take us to Heaven.

Ephesians 2:8–9

8   *For by grace are ye saved through faith; and that not of yourselves: it is the gift of God:*

9   *Not of works, lest any man should boast.*

The Bible says that it is only by grace that we will be saved from our sin and go to Heaven. Grace is God giving us something good that we don't deserve. And we surely don't deserve Heaven, because we are all sinners.

Romans 6:23a

23a For the wages of sin is death….

As sinners, we deserve death. That means that not only do we deserve for our bodies to die and be buried, but it also means that we deserve to go to the place the Bible calls Hell.

But God, in His wonderful grace, sent His Son, Jesus, to die for our sins so we wouldn't have to.

In order to have our sins forgiven and have a home in Heaven forever, we simply need to believe in Jesus and trust Him as our Saviour from sin. We need to have faith in Jesus.

The rich man had earthly riches—the money and comforts of this earth that cannot go with us when we die. Lazarus had heavenly riches—the riches that come through faith in Jesus and last forever and ever in Heaven.

What about you? Do you have heavenly riches? Have you accepted God's grace and trusted Jesus as your Saviour from sin? If you haven't chosen the heavenly riches, you can choose them right now, today. One of the teachers would be so happy to talk with you after class if you want to trust Jesus as your Saviour or learn more about what that means.

Do you remember the rich man's second request? He asked that Lazarus be sent to tell his brothers about Heaven and Hell. He didn't want his brothers to continue living their lives as he had lived his—ignoring God and His only way of salvation from sin. He wanted his brothers to hear the truth before it was too late for them.

Abraham told the rich man that if his brothers didn't believe the Bible and the preachers who have told them the truth, they wouldn't believe someone who returns from the dead, either.

That reminds those of you who have trusted Jesus as your Saviour from sin of a very important job you have. Your job is to tell others about the Saviour, so they can hear the truth and be saved from their sins.

Teaching Tip

Bring a supply of Gospel tracts with you to class. Pass them out and teach the students how to use them to witness. Encourage them to pass out tracts and to witness at every opportunity.

- You can give someone a tract.
- You can tell someone about how you trusted Jesus as your Saviour from sin.
- You can invite someone to church.
- You can write a letter telling about your salvation and include a Gospel tract in the envelope.
- There are many people with whom you can share the Gospel— friends at school, your parents, brothers and sisters, grandparents, uncles, aunts, and cousins, people you meet at the park or shopping.

Remember, heavenly riches, like Lazarus had, last for ever and ever, and now is the time to share them with others—before it's too late.

Correct or Consequences

Materials Needed

Game pieces for "Correct or Consequences" are found on the Ministry Resource CD.

Instructions

Choose a student to come to the front of the class and choose a "Correct or Consequence" card. Have him read the card containing a consequence to the class. Ask that student a review question. If the student answers correctly, the entire class performs the consequence on the card. If the student answers incorrectly, he alone must do the consequence on the card.

1. What is the name of the poor man in our story?
    Answer: Lazarus

2. What kind of clothing did the rich man wear?
    Answer: Purple and fine linen

3. Where did Lazarus wait and beg for food?
    Answer: At the rich man's gate.

4. What eventually happened to the poor man, and where did he go?
    Answer: He died and went to Heaven.

5. What eventually happened to the rich man, and where did he go?
    Answer: He died and went to Hell.

6. When the rich man looked up into Heaven, who were the two men he saw?
    Answer: Abraham and Lazarus

7. What two questions did the rich man ask Abraham?
    Answer: He asked for Lazarus to dip his finger in water and cool his tongue. He asked for Lazarus to tell his relatives about Jesus.

8. How did these two men's roles reverse in our story?
    Answer: See answers listed on page 137.

9. Even with all the rich man's money, could he purchase happiness that would last forever?

   Answer: No

10. What is a way that you can tell others about Jesus, so they can know how to go to Heaven?

    Answer: Answers will vary, but may include examples given from the lesson (page 139).

 # Teaching the Memory Verses

Ephesians 2:8–9

8   *For by grace are ye saved through faith; and that not of yourselves: it is the gift of God:*

9   *Not of works, lest any man should boast.*

Print flash cards and laminate for durability.

   Turn to Ephesians 2:8–9. Salvation is free for all who believe. We don't have to work for it, nor do we have to pay for it. When mom and dad give you a present on your birthday, they don't ask you to pay for it or bargain with you by saying that if you do all these chores then you can have it! They give it to you because they love you, and all you need to do is receive it.

   Introduce one flash card at a time. Show the class the first flash card and give them the correct wording of each picture. Then say this flash card together. Have a student come to the front and hold the flash card. Repeat with the rest of the flash cards.

Object Lesson—Going to Heaven!

Materials Needed:

- Balloons
- Paper Plate
- Salt and Pepper

Lesson:

Blow up a balloon (no need for helium). Bring a paper plate or pan and salt and pepper. Explain that the balloon will represent Heaven. Sprinkle the salt onto the plate. Tell the group that the salt stands for the rich man. Now sprinkle pepper onto the plate. Explain that the pepper represents Lazarus. Now rub the balloon in your hair (or someone else's hair) to create static electricity. Put the balloon up to the plate. Instantly, the pepper will cling to the balloon, while the salt stays on the plate.

Share how Lazarus went to Heaven because he believed in Jesus, and the rich man did not go to Heaven because he did not believe. Explain how a person can go to Heaven. Let students try the trick with extra balloons.

Additional Resources

Find the following items on the Ministry Resource CD:

- Coloring Page (for younger children)
- Activity Page (for older children)
- Student Take-Home Paper
- PowerPoint Presentation

Craft—Invitation

Getting It Together

Ribbon
Hole punch
Colored paper

Per student:
1   clear bag
1   tract
1   craft template from the Ministry Resource CD

Putting It Together

1.   Print and cut out the Lesson 9 craft verse template.
2.   Hole punch a hole in the top left corner of the verse.
3.   Put ribbon at the bottom of the clear bag.
4.   Put your church's tract in the bag.
5.   Tie the bag with ribbon.
6.   String ribbon through the verse and tie it to the bag.

Seeing It Together

God has given us an invitation to accept Him into our lives! Now, we should share that invitation with others. This week give this invitation you made today to someone else who needs to hear about the love of Jesus.

Suggested Classroom Schedule

Before Class	Complete attendance record. Provide students with coloring/activity pages.
Opening	Welcome
Prayer	Prayer requests and praise reports from the children
Song Time	
Memory Verse	James 4:10
Song Time	
Object Lesson	A Real Christian
Bible Lesson	The Two Men Who Prayed
Application/Invitation	Help saved students apply lesson. Invite unsaved students to receive Christ.
Snack	Pretzels
Review Game/ Questions	Star Points
Craft	Prayer Magnet
Closing	Give announcements and pray. Distribute take-home papers.

Lesson Ten Overview

The Two Men Who Prayed

Theme—Prayer is a privilege.

Scripture
Luke 18:9–14

Memory Verse
James 4:10—*"Humble yourselves in the sight of the Lord, and he shall lift you up."*

Lesson Outline

Introducing the Story
In the story we will hear today, Jesus tells us about how God looks at proud people.

Telling the Story
1. **The Two Men Go to Pray** *(v. 10)*
2. **The Proud Pharisee** *(vv. 11–12)—Flash Card 10.1*
3. **The Humble Publican** *(v. 13)—Flash Card 10.2*

Jesus Explains the Story *(Matthew 6:5, James 4:6b, 1 Peter 5:5b–6)—Flash Card 10.3*

Applying the Story *(Matthew 5:3,5, Proverbs 22:4, 1 John 1:9, Psalm 139:23–24, Psalm 19:14)*
Are you a proud or a humble person? A humble person is the happiest person of all!

10 Lesson Ten

The Two Men Who Prayed

Theme: Prayer is a privilege.

 ## Scripture

Luke 18:9–14

9 And he spake this parable unto certain which trusted in themselves that they were righteous, and despised others:

10 Two men went up into the temple to pray; the one a Pharisee, and the other a publican.

11 The Pharisee stood and prayed thus with himself, God, I thank thee, that I am not as other men are, extortioners, unjust, adulterers, or even as this publican.

12 I fast twice in the week, I give tithes of all that I possess.

13 And the publican, standing afar off, would not lift up so much as his eyes unto heaven, but smote upon his breast, saying, God be merciful to me a sinner.

14 I tell you, this man went down to his house justified rather than the other: for every one that exalteth himself shall be abased; and he that humbleth himself shall be exalted.

Memory Verse

James 4:10
"Humble yourselves in the sight of the Lord, and he shall lift you up."

Teacher's Checklist

- ❑ Read Luke 18:9–14 daily.

- ❑ Study Lesson 10.

- ❑ Flash cards 10.1–10.3

- ❑ Prepare snack—pretzels.

- ❑ Gather for lesson—glass of water, carrot, and salt.

- ❑ Print and cut out "Star Points" review game from the Ministry Resource CD.

- ❑ Print this week's memory verse (James 4:10) from the Ministry Resource CD.

- ❑ Gather for object lesson—clown nose, mustache, friendly mask, something to disguise a child.

- ❑ Purchase for craft per student—clothespin, magnet, foam letters that spell "Pray."

- ❑ Print for craft—1 set of prayer cards per student from the Ministry Resource CD.

- ❑ Gather for craft—cardstock, scissors.

- ❑ Print and duplicate Coloring Pages or Activity Pages on the Ministry Resource CD (one per student).

- ❑ Print and duplicate Take-Home Paper on the Ministry Resource CD (one per student).

Bible Lesson

Scripture: Luke 18:9–14

INTRODUCING THE STORY

Sometimes when Jesus taught people, He would read or quote to them from the Bible. Jesus knew many people were interested in what the Bible said, and that many of them wanted to follow the Bible.

Other times, when Jesus wanted people to learn about Him, He would do a miracle. Sometimes His miracle would be healing a lame man or a blind person. Sometimes His miracle would be feeding thousands of people from a lunch only big enough for one person. One time His miracle was to make water into juice at a wedding. When Jesus performed a miracle, it showed that He was really God. It showed that Jesus had power to cause events to happen differently than they naturally would.

There were some people who, it seemed, wouldn't learn through Bible teaching. These people didn't want to see miracles, either, because they didn't want to believe that Jesus really was God. These people who wouldn't listen to the Bible and weren't interested in miracles were proud people who trusted in themselves.

Now, when a proud person would come to Jesus, the proud person usually wanted to prove to Jesus that he was right and Jesus was wrong, which, of course, he could never do. Proud people often argued with Jesus. Can you imagine arguing with Jesus?

Jesus understood proud people. He knew that a proud person always thinks he's right. He knew that a proud person thinks he is better than other people and that his way is better than other people's way. He knew that a proud person usually won't listen to the Bible if it doesn't agree with his own thoughts.

So, when some proud people came to Jesus one day, He knew just what to do. Jesus always knows the right and best thing to do. The proud people who came to Jesus this day loved themselves and their goodness. Not only did they love themselves, but they hated everyone else. They thought they were better than anyone else.

"There is one way to show them their need," Jesus may have thought. "There is one way to let them see the truth about proud people. I will tell them a story that shows them exactly what they are like. This story will show them how God looks at proud people."

THE STORY

1. Two Men Go to Pray (v. 10)

Two men, each very different from the other, headed toward the temple. One, a Pharisee—a religious ruler who thought he was better than other people—walked with his head held high. The other, a publican—a tax collector who was disliked by many people because he came to them to collect their taxes—cheerfully greeted the people he met along the way. Both men were on their way to pray.

"Ah, what a fine day to go to the temple," the Pharisee thought to himself as he hurried toward the temple. "The sun is shining, the birds are singing, and many people will be there today. I need to hurry, so I can arrive while the crowds are still there. I want there to be a lot of people to hear my prayers!"

"What a beautiful day God has given us," the publican thought, on his way toward the temple. "I'm thankful I can go to the temple, since God told us in His Word that it is important that we go there regularly. I don't deserve for God to love me, but I'm so glad He does!"

The Pharisee and the publican arrived at the temple at the same time.

Flash Card 10.1

2. The Proud Pharisee (vv. 11–12)

"It's good to be able to show people what a fine religious man I am," the Pharisee thought as he hurried to the front of the temple. "I'm glad I have such a good education and a splendid ability in public speaking." As he stood at the front, he began to pray out loud.

"God," the Pharisee cried out, "I thank you that I am not like other men. Thank you that I am so much better than other men. Thank you that I am not an extortioner—I don't force people to pay what they owe. I don't trick people. Why, I would never do that. I'm so gracious and kind. I'm a very religious man."

"Thank you, God," he cried, a little louder this time to make sure all the people heard, "that I am not unjust—I'm not dishonest. Why, I would never be dishonest. I follow the law exactly. I'm a very religious man."

"Thank you, also, God," he cried, "that I am a faithful husband. I would not be unfaithful to my wife, for I am a very religious man."

"Another thing I thank you for, God, is that I am not like this publican here." As he spoke these words, the Pharisee looked scornfully at the publican, and then he continued. "Nobody likes a publican. Why, I imagine he even takes more money than he should from people when he is collecting taxes. Just look at him—standing there at the back of the temple. He's not even worthy to come up to the front, like I am. I am so much better than this publican. I am a very religious man."

The Pharisee smiled to himself as he thought about how bad the publican probably was. "Why, this publican's badness makes me look really good," he thought in his heart.

"And, thank you God that I do all my religious duties," the Pharisee cried out, peeking around to make sure no one had turned their attention away from him. "Two days a week I fast in order to prove what a religious man I am. Not only that, but I give tithes of everything I own. That shows everyone what a good religious man I really am. Thank you God, that I am so good!"

3. The Humble Publican (v. 13)

At the same time the Pharisee was praying, the publican was also praying. But his prayer was very different. The publican bowed his head and prayed, "Dear Lord, You are so good to listen to my prayers. Thank You that You are a God of love, and especially that You love me! Thank You that, even though I don't deserve it, You forgive me of my sin. I feel like the worst sinner in the world, and yet You forgive me. I am so sorry for my sin. I have nothing in me that makes me worthy to come to you, Lord. There is nothing good in me. But You are all good. And You have told us to come to You and ask for Your mercy."

As the publican prayed, he felt unworthy to talk to God. As he thought about his sin, he clasped his hands across his chest, and he began pounding his chest with his fists. "Forgive me, Lord," he prayed. "Be merciful to me, dear Lord. You are so great, and I am so unworthy of Your love and forgiveness."

JESUS EXPLAINS THE STORY

Jesus turned toward the proud people who were listening to His story. They were beginning to feel uncomfortable—they knew why Jesus told the story, and they were beginning to see how foolish pride looked. The humble publican was justified. God looked at him just as if he had never sinned. He went home happy and forgiven. He knew He needed God's forgiveness and mercy, and he asked for it.

Flash Card 10.2

💡 **Teaching Tip**

As you describe the publican's prayer, demonstrate the intensity, even pounding your chest with your fists as you plead for mercy. This will help contextualize this as a gesture of humility.

Flash Card 10.3

"But the proud Pharisee," Jesus went on, "didn't see he needed forgiveness. He went back home to his house just the way he had come—proud, selfish, and unforgiven."

Matthew 6:5

5   And when thou prayest, thou shalt not be as the hypocrites are: for they love to pray standing in the synagogues and in the corners of the streets, that they may be seen of men. Verily I say unto you, They have their reward.

A person who lifts himself up will be brought down, but a person who humbles himself will be lifted up and blessed.

James 4:6b

6b   God resisteth the proud, but giveth grace unto the humble.

1 Peter 5:5b–6

5b   God resisteth the proud, and giveth grace to the humble.

6   Humble yourselves therefore under the mighty hand of God, that he may exalt you in due time.

APPLYING THE STORY

A humble person is the happiest person of all.

Matthew 5:3, 5

3   Blessed [happy] are the poor in spirit: for their's is the kingdom of heaven.

5   Blessed [happy] are the meek: for they shall inherit the earth.

Proverbs 22:4

4   By humility and the fear of the LORD are riches, and honour, and life.

A humble person knows that he or she needs God, because God made him or her and God knows what is best.

A humble person knows:

- God is always right.
- God is always good.
- God created him and knows what is best for him.
- He is a sinner who needs God's mercy.
- He needs God and God's wisdom for everything he does and every decision he has to make.
- He is no better than anyone else.
- He is no worse than anyone else.
- He has much to learn.
- He is not in control of his own life.
- He has authorities to obey—God, parents, pastor, and teachers.

A proud person, on the other hand, isn't really happy in his heart. God created us to obey and honor Him, and when we don't, we are unhappy. A proud person:

- Wants to do his own thing.
- Wants to go his own way.
- Often compares himself to others.
- Thinks he is better than others.
- Often makes fun of others in order to make himself look better.
- Thinks he is always right.
- Won't take correction from God or other authorities.
- Is often angry when he doesn't get his own way.
- Doesn't let the Bible show him that he is wrong.
- Doesn't often have time for God.
- Doesn't confess his sin to God.
- Thinks about himself more than pleasing others and pleasing God.
- Doesn't usually have many friends, because people don't want to spend time with someone who thinks he is always right and who thinks he is better than they are.

 **Teaching Tip**

Draw your students' attention to the Pharisee's prayer. Note the fact that he used the personal pronoun "I" five times in his two-verse prayer. Encourage your students to notice if they speak more of *I* or of *you, we, he, she,* and *they*. This can often be a signal to us as to whether our thoughts are prideful or humble.

Did you see yourself in Jesus' story? For those of us who have pride in our lives (and that is usually most of us), Jesus told this story just for us. Jesus is very kind to show us what we need in our lives so we can go to Him, asking for forgiveness. When we tell Him we know we have sinned, and what our sins are, He says He will forgive us and cleanse us.

1 John 1:9

9   *If we confess our sins, he is faithful and just to forgive us our sins, and to cleanse us from all unrighteousness.*

When we ask God to forgive us, we go, in one moment's time, from being proud to being humble! God forgives and cleanses us immediately. Then we can keep going to Jesus, spending time with Him, and asking Him to keep pride out of our hearts.

If you haven't been thinking, living, and acting like the proud Pharisee, or if you have asked God to forgive you for your pride, God shows you exactly how to continue putting Him first and how to have a humble spirit:

- Give God and His Word first place in your life.
- Every day ask God to show you the sin in your heart and life. Then, ask Him to forgive you and cleanse you.

Psalm 139:23–24

23   *Search me, O God, and know my heart: try me, and know my thoughts:*

24   *And see if there be any wicked way in me, and lead me in the way everlasting.*

- Thank God for His goodness to you.
- Thank Him for salvation, your family, and your church.
- Ask Him to keep you from being tempted and from sin.
- Ask Him to meet all your needs.
- Pray for other people.
- Ask God to give you His thoughts and to help you do His ways.

Psalm 19:14

14   *Let the words of my mouth, and the meditation of my heart, be acceptable in thy sight, O LORD, my strength, and my redeemer.*

These are steps to living a happy, humble life like the publican in Jesus' story.

Review Game/Questions

Star Points

Materials Needed
Print "Star Points" game pieces from the Ministry Resource CD.

Instructions
Print and cut game pieces. Laminate for durability. Place game pieces in a bag. Divide the class into two teams.

Ask Team 1 a review question. If the student answers correctly, he may pull out a game piece from the bag. There should be a letter on the star. Count how many times that letter appears in today's memory verse. Multiply that number by 100 and that is the amount of points for that turn. (e.g. Student draws an "H." The letter "H" appears six times. This team gets 600 points.)

1. What two men went to the temple to pray?
   Answer: A Pharisee and a publican

2. What is a Pharisee?
   Answer: A Pharisee was a religious ruler who thought he was better than other people.

3. What is a publican?
   Answer: A publican was a tax collector who was disliked by many people because he had to collect their money.

4. How did the Pharisee pray to God in the temple?
   Answer: He displayed pride by praying loudly so everyone could hear him.

5. What did the Pharisee pray?
   Answer: He thanked God that he was not like the publican.

6. How did the publican pray to God?
   Answer: He bowed his head and quietly prayed with humility.

7. What did the publican pray?
   Answer: He asked for forgiveness and mercy.

8. What happens if you try to exalt yourself, like the Pharisee did?
   Answer: You will be brought low.

9. What will happen if you humble yourself before the Lord?
   Answer: He will lift you up.

10. How can you display a humble spirit?
    Answer: Answers will vary, but may include examples given on page 152.

Teaching the Memory Verse

James 4:10

10   Humble yourselves in the sight of the Lord, and he shall lift you up.

Have students open their Bibles to James 4:10.

Being humble does not mean that you are sad and walk with your head down all the time, but it does mean that you don't focus on yourself. We need to be careful not to always say "I" or "me." We shouldn't draw attention to ourselves, but to the Lord instead. God honors those who have a humble spirit.

Help the students get into pairs and have them teach each other the verse. Take time for the students to recite the verse to the class.

Object Lesson—A Real Christian

Materials Needed:
- Clown nose
- Mustache
- Friendly mask
- Something to disguise a child

Lesson:

Have a child come forward, and place the disguise or mask on the child. Before you place the mask on, ask the child to tell the entire class his name. After you place the mask on his face, tell him he is now called, "_____" (whatever is a good name for the mask or disguise). Ask the class what the person's name is. The class will more than likely answer with the child's real name. Explain to the children that it doesn't matter what you put on or pretend to be, you will always be the same person inside. Help them understand that just because someone acts right and talks right doesn't mean they have a walk with Christ. Some people try to disguise themselves as good people. Encourage your students to live genuine Christian lives of humility.

Craft—Prayer Magnet

Getting It Together

Cardstock

Scissors

Per student:

Foam craft letters that spell "Pray"

1   clothespin

1   magnet

1   set of prayer cards from the Ministry Resource CD

Putting It Together

1. Print and cut out the prayer cards located on the Ministry Resource CD.
2. Glue the magnet to the back of the clothespin.
3. Stick or glue the prayer letters to the front of the clothespin.
4. Clip the prayer cards together using the clothespin.

Seeing It Together

God wants each of us to pray to Him from a humble heart! Use these prayer cards to remind you to pray for yourself and others.

Additional Resources

Find the following items on the Ministry Resource CD:

*   Coloring Page (for younger children)

*   Activity Page (for older children)

*   Student Take-Home Paper

*   PowerPoint Presentation

Suggested Classroom Schedule

Before Class	Complete attendance record. Provide students with coloring/activity pages.
Opening	Welcome
Prayer	Prayer requests and praise reports from the children
Song Time	
Memory Verse	Psalm 68:19
Song Time	
Object Lesson	No Loitering Allowed
Bible Lesson	The Hired Laborers
Application/Invitation	Help saved students apply lesson. Invite unsaved students to receive Christ.
Snack	Grapes
Review Game/ Questions	M & M Relay
Craft	Penny
Closing	Give announcements and pray. Distribute take-home papers.

Lesson Eleven Overview

The Hired Laborers

Theme—Good gifts come from God.

Scripture

Matthew 20:1–16

Memory Verse

Psalm 68:19—"Blessed be the Lord, who daily loadeth us with benefits, even the God of our salvation. Selah."

Lesson Outline

Introducing the Story

Jesus' disciples wanted to know how they would be rewarded for all they had done for Jesus. Jesus began yet another story about a farmer. Let's open up our Bibles and see how Jesus answers His disciples.

Telling the Story

1. The Grape Harvest (v. 1)

2. The Farmer Goes to Hire Laborers (vv. 2–7) —Flash Card 11.1, 11.2

3. The Laborers' Paychecks (vv. 8–10)

4. The Angry Laborers (vv. 11–12)—Flash Card 11.3

5. The Farmer's Answer (vv. 13–16)

Jesus Explains the Story (Job 12:13)

Applying the Story (Romans 12:15, Psalm 145:9a,15, Matthew 5:45b, James 1:17)

Just as the laborers could only receive what the farmer paid them, you and I can only receive what we are given by God.

11 Lesson Eleven

The Hired Laborers

Theme: Good gifts come from God.

 ## Scripture

Matthew 20:1–16

1 *For the kingdom of heaven is like unto a man that is an householder, which went out early in the morning to hire labourers into his vineyard.*

2 *And when he had agreed with the labourers for a penny a day, he sent them into his vineyard.*

3 *And he went out about the third hour, and saw others standing idle in the marketplace,*

4 *And said unto them; Go ye also into the vineyard, and whatsoever is right I will give you. And they went their way.*

5 *Again he went out about the sixth and ninth hour, and did likewise.*

6 *And about the eleventh hour he went out, and found others standing idle, and saith unto them, Why stand ye here all the day idle?*

7 *They say unto him, Because no man hath hired us. He saith unto them, Go ye also into the vineyard; and whatsoever is right, that shall ye receive.*

8 *So when even was come, the lord of the vineyard saith unto his steward, Call the labourers, and give them their hire, beginning from the last unto the first.*

9 *And when they came that were hired about the eleventh hour, they received every man a penny.*

10 *But when the first came, they supposed that they should have received more; and they likewise received every man a penny.*

11 *And when they had received it, they murmured against the goodman of the house,*

12 *Saying, These last have wrought but one hour, and thou hast made them equal unto us, which have borne the burden and heat of the day.*

13 *But he answered one of them, and said, Friend, I do thee no wrong: didst not thou agree with me for a penny?*

Memory Verse

Psalm 68:19
"Blessed be the Lord, who daily loadeth us with benefits, even the God of our salvation. Selah."

14 *Take that thine is, and go thy way: I will give unto this last, even as unto thee.*

15 *Is it not lawful for me to do what I will with mine own? Is thine eye evil, because I am good?*

16 *So the last shall be first, and the first last: for many be called, but few chosen.*

Teacher's Checklist

❑ Read Matthew 20:1–16 daily.

❑ Study Lesson 11.

❑ Flash cards 11.1–11.3

❑ Prepare snack—grapes.

❑ Gather for review game—glass, M & M's, straws.

❑ Print this week's memory verse from the Ministry Resource CD.

❑ Make sign for object lesson.

❑ Print for craft—Penny template from the Ministry Resource CD (one per student).

❑ Gather for craft—glue, scissors, white cardstock.

❑ Print and duplicate Coloring Pages or Activity Pages on the Ministry Resource CD (one per student).

❑ Print and duplicate Take-Home Paper on the Ministry Resource CD (one per student).

Grapes
God blesses us with good gifts. As the children eat their grapes, discuss the story and have them list some "good gifts."

Bible Lesson

Scripture: Matthew 20:1–16

INTRODUCING THE STORY

Have you ever been paid to do a job? Maybe you are given an allowance for keeping your room clean, doing the dishes, or taking care of the dog. Maybe you have been paid for helping to clean out the garage, mowing the lawn, or shoveling snow for your neighbor.

Most of the time, when you are hired to do a particular job, the person who hires you tells you ahead of time how much he or she is going to pay you. The pay you receive for your work is your reward for the job you have done.

One time, Peter, Jesus' disciple, wanted to remind Jesus that he and the other disciples had been doing the very important job of following Him. They had been serving the Lord faithfully, and Peter wanted to know how they would be rewarded for all they had done for Jesus. "We have forsaken all, and followed thee; what shall we have therefore?" (Matthew 19:27). Peter asked Jesus. "We have given up everything and spent our lives working for you. Now, what will our pay, or our reward, be?" Peter could hardly wait to hear Jesus' answer.

"I have a story for all of you," Jesus said. And He began yet another story about a farmer—the parable of "The Labourers in the Vineyard."

Teaching Tip

Ask your students to briefly tell of jobs for which they have been paid. Ask if it was a regularly scheduled job or a one-time happening. You can never find out too much about the daily lives of your students, and it is very meaningful to them when, later on, you remember what they have shared with you.

THE STORY

1. The Grape Harvest (v. 1)

The farmer was a good man. He worked hard to build a pleasant, sturdy home for his wife and children. He raised sheep, cows, and chickens. He planted wheat, barley, and grapes.

One morning late in the summer, the farmer sat at breakfast with his wife. "The grape harvest is ready, and God has given us an abundant crop this year," he said. "If I don't get all the grapes harvested today, I'm afraid they will spoil on the vines. I'm just not sure I can do it all alone, though."

The farmer's good wife said, "You've been working so hard all summer. And you're right—God has blessed us. You're also right that there are too many grapes for you to harvest alone. Why don't you go down to the marketplace and hire some men to help you? It's still early in the morning, and if you go right away, I think you could get all the grapes harvested today. You just need some men to help you."

"Thank you, dear," the farmer said, as he kissed his wife and hurried off to the marketplace. "That's exactly what I'll do."

2. The Farmer Goes to Hire Laborers (vv. 2–7)

Flash Card 11.1

It was about 6:00 in the morning, and the sun was just beginning to rise as the farmer neared the marketplace. "Good—there are many hours left in this day," the farmer thought. "I think my wife was right—I think we can get all those grapes harvested before sundown, if we start right away and work our hardest."

There were a few men standing in the marketplace. They had brought their tools, and they were hoping for someone to hire them. "Come with me to my vineyard," the farmer said. "The grapes are heavy on the vine. I'll pay you each a full day's wages for helping me harvest my grapes."

Happy to have a job for the whole day, the men followed the farmer to his vineyard.

The farmer and his hired men worked as hard and as fast as they could. The sun was rising higher in the sky, and the farmer could see the day was passing quickly. About 9:00 in the morning, the farmer said to his hired men, "There are too many grapes for us to harvest without more help. I'm going back to the marketplace to see if there are any more men who can help us."

When the farmer arrived at the marketplace, he saw some men standing there. "I am harvesting grapes in my vineyard today, and there are too many for me to harvest without more help. Hurry to my vineyard, and at the end of the day I will pay you whatever is right."

The men in the marketplace had heard of the farmer. Every one around knew he was an honest man who paid his workers well. The men, happy for a job, hurried off to the vineyard.

Now the farmer had many workers helping him to harvest his grapes. But, at about noon, the farmer looked at the hot sun, high in the sky. "This day is almost half over, and we're not half done harvesting grapes," the farmer thought to himself. As quickly as he could, the farmer hurried off to the marketplace to find more laborers.

"If you come help us harvest the grapes in my vineyard, I'll pay you what is right at the end of the day," the farmer told the men who were standing in the marketplace. These men were so happy, as they had been afraid that no one would hire them, since it was now late in the day. They agreed, picked up their tools, and followed the farmer to his vineyard.

At 3:00 in the afternoon, the farmer thought to himself, "I just didn't realize how many grapes there actually are! I have been greatly blessed of God—so much so that I need more workers." He rushed to the marketplace and hurried back with a few more workers. "Surely I have enough workers now," the farmer said.

Flash Card 11.2

Now the farmer had men working in every part of his vineyard. Everyone was busy, cutting big clusters of grapes, and placing them in his basket. When the basket was full, the worker would run and get another basket, cut grapes, and place them into the basket. They worked like this all day long.

At 5:00 in the evening, the farmer looked at the sky. "It will be dark soon," he thought. "With just a few more workers, I think we would actually be able to finish the harvest. I doubt, though, that there will be any men at the marketplace looking for work. The day's almost over, and surely they have all gone home. It's worth a try though—it's my only hope of finishing the harvest today, before it's too late." With that, the farmer headed off toward the marketplace.

There were some men at the marketplace. "Why are you just standing here, doing nothing?" the farmer asked the men.

"No one has hired us," they all answered at once.

"Well, go to my vineyard and help us finish up the grape harvest. At the end of the day I will pay you whatever is right."

"Can you believe it?" the men excitedly asked each other as they ran off to the vineyard. "We thought it was too late in the day—we thought no one would hire us, and we didn't think we would have money to buy the things we need. But, now, the farmer has hired us. This is a very good day!"

The last group of men labored in the farmer's vineyard for the final hour of the day. And, sure enough, at 6:00, the grape harvest was finished! The farmer was so happy.

3. The Laborers' Paychecks (vv. 8–10)

The farmer called his servant to him. "It's time to pay the laborers I have hired for the day," the farmer said. "Make sure you thank them for their hard work. Give each man a full day's wages."

The servant called all the laborers to him. "You have been a great help to the farmer," the servant said gratefully. "He couldn't have finished the harvest without you men. Thank you for giving your best and working your hardest. Now, it's time for you to receive your pay."

The servant first went to the men the farmer had hired at 5:00 in the evening—the last men who had been hired. The men had never worked for such a short time before, and they didn't know what to expect. "What?!" they exclaimed as the servant handed them an entire day's wages. "Oh, thank you! We never thought we would get paid for a whole day's work, when we have only worked one hour."

"Can you believe that?!" the men who had been hired at 6:00 in the morning excitedly exclaimed to each other. "We have worked all day in the hot sun. We have labored and sweated all day, and we will soon be paid. We have worked so much longer than these last men, and if they were paid for a whole day's work, just think how much we will be paid!" These first men could hardly wait. They just knew they were going to be paid much more than they had been promised.

4. The Angry Laborers (vv. 11–12)

Flash Card 11.3

The excitement of these first men quickly turned to disappointment, and their disappointment turned to anger. As the servant thanked them and handed them each a day's wages, the men complained to him. They said, "These last men have only worked one hour, and you have paid them the same amount you are paying us. We started work early this morning—at 6:00! We worked hard all day, with the sun beating down on our backs. Surely we should be paid much more than these last men who have hardly worked at all. It's just not fair!"

5. The Farmer's Answer (vv. 13–16)

The good farmer was listening sadly as these men complained to his servant. "Friends," the farmer kindly said to the men. "I am not doing wrong to you. In fact, I've been good to you. I have hired you and paid you just as I said I would. Didn't you agree to work all day for a day's wages? I have paid you exactly what I promised. And, I have chosen to give to these last men the same as I have given to you.

"Don't you think I can do as I wish with my own money? Are you jealous* because I am kind to the men I hired last? I have not been unfair. I have given you what I promised, and I have been kind to the others as well."

JESUS EXPLAINS THE STORY

Do you remember why Jesus told the parable of The Laborers in the Vineyard? (Allow time for students' responses.) He was answering Peter's question about what the disciples would receive as a reward for following Jesus.

Peter had thought that, since the disciples had followed Jesus so faithfully, surely they we would be given great reward. Jesus told the story to let Peter know that, yes, they had followed and served the Lord. And, yes, they would be rewarded, but maybe the rewards wouldn't be exactly like they thought. Jesus wanted to remind Peter that God is good, and He has the right to decide to reward each person as He chooses, not necessarily as they think they deserve.

Teacher's Note

*The text says, "Is thine eye evil, because I am good?" (Matthew 20:15).
"An evil eye" was a phrase in use among the ancient Jews, to denote an envious, covetous man or disposition; a man who repined at his neighbour's prosperity, loved his own money, and would do nothing in the way of charity for God's sake." (*Adam Clarke's Bible Commentary*)

Job 12:13

13   With him is wisdom and strength, he hath counsel
       and understanding.

You see, the farmer rewarded all of his workers. Some thought they would receive a little, and some thought they would receive a lot. And they all received at least as much as the farmer had promised them. The ones who worked the most received exactly what they had been promised, and the ones who worked the least received just as much as the others—because the good farmer decided to show kindness to them.

The farmer was not unfair to any of his workers. You see, those who were hired first thought they deserved more than those who were hired last. After all, they had worked much longer and harder. But, the truth is, when they were hired early in the morning, they knew they would work a whole day and receive the whole day's pay. It was worth it to them to work one day for one day's pay, so they accepted the job the farmer offered them.

But, when they saw those who had worked only one hour receive as much as they received, they thought the farmer was unfair, and they became jealous. They didn't realize that the farmer wasn't unfair to them—he simply was gracious to those who had worked only one hour. It was the good farmer's right to be extra kind to whomever he chose.

APPLYING THE STORY

Just as the laborers could only receive what the farmer paid them, you and I can only receive what we are given by God. And, just as the laborers had the choice of how to feel about their rewards, we have that choice as well.

The men who were hired early in the morning would have been much happier if they would have been glad for the men who received a whole day's pay for only one hour's work. They could have thought, "Wow! The farmer is so kind to those men! I'm glad to work for such a generous man." If the first laborers had thought about the farmer's generosity, they would have been grateful for what they did receive, and they would have been happy for the last laborers, who received just as much. They wouldn't have had those awful feelings of jealousy making them miserable in their hearts. They had a choice.

Romans 12:15

15   *Rejoice with them that do rejoice, and weep with them that weep.*

How do you feel when someone gets a privilege or gift you were hoping for?

- You had been wanting a puppy for months or years, and your friend got a puppy, but you didn't.

Teaching Tip

Add examples from the reservoir of observations you have made over the weeks of teaching your particular students. Choose illustrations that relate to your students' desires and aspirations.

- Someone else was given the part you were hoping for in the church Christmas program.
- You saw a pair of shoes you really liked, but your mom said they were too expensive. The next day, your friend was wearing that exact pair of shoes.
- Your friend has a bigger and newer house than your family's house.
- You were hoping for the job of mowing your neighbor's lawn, but the boy in the house across the street was given the job instead of you.
- You wanted to sing in a trio at church, but someone was chosen instead of you.

From Jesus' parable, we learn that the best thing to do when someone else is blessed is to rejoice with them! We can choose to be happy that their God is our God, and that He is very generous. If God is generous to them, we can know that He will also be generous to us.

Psalm 145:9a, 15

9a   *The LORD is good to all….*

15   *The eyes of all wait upon thee; and thou givest them their meat in due season.*

If you think, "But they don't deserve it, and I do," that gives you even more reason to be glad for them.

Matthew 5:45b

45b   *[He] maketh his sun to rise on the evil and on the good, and sendeth rain on the just and on the unjust.*

Just think—you serve a God who gives people good things that they don't deserve (that's called *grace*). Not only does He give other people good things they don't deserve, but He also gives you good things that you don't deserve. That's something to rejoice about!

James 1:17

17   *Every good gift, and every perfect gift is from above, and cometh down from the Father of lights, with whom is no variableness, neither shadow of turning.*

Teaching Tip

Close the lesson by playing an alphabet thankfulness game. Have each student say, "God's so good to me. He has blessed me with something that begins with *A*." Continue going around the room until you have completed the entire alphabet.

M & M Relay
Materials Needed
- 1 empty glass
- Bowl of M & M's
- Straws

Instructions
Put the bowl of M & M's on one end of the table and the empty glass at the other end.

When students correctly answer a review question, they come to the front. Using the straw (not their hands) they suck up one M & M and carry it (by the straw only) to the other end of the table and drop in the glass. They try to get as many M & M's into the glass within one minute. They get to eat the M & M's that are in the glass. Keep score of who holds the record.

1. What kind of help did the farmer need?
   Answer: He needed laborers to help him harvest his vineyard.

2. What time of day did the farmer go to the marketplace?
   Answer: Early in the morning

3. How much money did the first group of men agree to be paid?
   Answer: One penny for the day's work

4. When the farmer went out to hire workers the final three times, did they know how much they would be paid?
   Answer: No

5. How much did the workers in the last three groups receive for their work?
   Answer: One penny

6. Why did some of the workers complain about their payment?
   Answer: Because the work time was not equal, but the pay was.

7. Was the farmer unfair to his laborers?
   Answer: No. He was simply gracious to those who had worked only one hour.

8. What is the best thing we can do when someone else is blessed?
    Answer: Rejoice with them!

9. Who is the giver of everything we have?
    Answer: God

10. What does "grace" mean?
    Answer: Giving something to someone who does not deserve it.

 # Teaching the Memory Verse

Psalm 68:19

19   Blessed be the Lord, who daily loadeth us with benefits, even the God of our salvation. Selah.

Print flash card and laminate for durability. Have the students open their Bibles to Psalm 68:19.

God provides us with daily blessings, and His blessings are generous!

Amen!

Read the verse together several times; then ask the students to close their Bibles. Instruct the students to stand, and explain the order in which they will recite the following verse in the following manner: The first student begins by stating the reference, "Psalm 68:19." The second child then says, "Blessed," followed by the third child who says, "be." Continue this process until the last word is said. After the last word is said, the next student says "Amen," and the following person has to sit down. For the first round help the students with their word, but after a few practice rounds, the student that cannot say their word needs to sit, as well. The last person standing is the winner!

Object Lesson—No Loitering Allowed

Materials Needed:
"No Loitering Allowed" sign

For the Teacher:
The object you will use for this lesson will be a "No Loitering Allowed" sign. (You can make one yourself or print one from the computer. You might even want to print off several different signs to show your students.)

To the Class:
Ask the following questions to help stimulate discussion:

1. What am I holding? (Wait for a response such as "a 'no loitering' sign.")

2. That's right. What does it mean to loiter? (Wait for responses.) The dictionary says that to loiter means: "to linger aimlessly, to move in a slow, idle manner, making purposeless stops in the course of a trip, journey, errand, to waste time or dawdle over work."

3. Why would stores or certain places put up this sign? (Wait for responses.)

The men in our story were loitering in the marketplace until someone came and hired them. When the day was over, some of the men complained about their wages. They were not thankful for what they had been given.

God blessed the men in this parable by providing them with work! Though some were not thankful for their pay, they made more money by working than they would have made by loitering all day! Let's remember that God is good and that all we have comes from Him! And let's also stay busy doing His work!

Getting It Together

Glue
Scissors
White cardstock

Per student:
1   Penny template from the Ministry
    Resource CD

Putting It Together

1.   Print and cut out Penny template located on the Ministry
     Resource CD.
2.   Glue the front and back together.

Seeing It Together

Remind the students that everything they own belongs to the Lord.

 Additional Resources

Find the following items on the Ministry Resource CD:

•   Coloring Page (for younger children)

•   Activity Page (for older children)

•   Student Take-Home Paper

•   PowerPoint Presentation

Suggested Classroom Schedule

Before Class	Complete attendance record. Provide students with coloring/activity pages.
Opening	Welcome
Prayer	Prayer requests and praise reports from the children
Song Time	
Memory Verse	Matthew 28:19
Song Time	
Object Lesson	You're Invited!
Bible Lesson	The Wedding Guests
Application/Invitation	Help saved students apply lesson. Invite unsaved students to receive Christ.
Snack	Wedding Cake
Review Game/Questions	Pin the Points on the Map
Craft	Sweetheart List
Closing	Give announcements and pray. Distribute take-home papers.

Lesson Twelve Overview

The Wedding Guests
Theme—Tell others about Jesus.

Scripture
Matthew 22:1–14

Memory Verse
Matthew 28:19— *"Go ye therefore, and teach all nations, baptizing them in the name of the Father, and of the Son, and of the Holy Ghost."*

Lesson Outline
Introducing the Story
Today's story is about a wedding invitation from Jesus. Let's find out if the people were as excited to receive a wedding invitation as we would be.

Telling the Story
1. **The First Group of Invitations Given and Refused** (v. 3)—*Flash Card 12.1*

2. **The Second Group of Invitations Given and Refused** (vv. 4–5)

3. **The Servants Beaten and Killed** (v. 6)

4. **The King's Armies Commissioned** (v. 7)

5. **Everyone Given a Wedding Invitation** (vv. 8–10)

6. **The Wedding Filled with Guests** (v. 10) — *Flash Card 12.2*

7. **The Guest Without a Wedding Garment** (v. 11–14) — *Flash Card 12.3*

Applying the Story (*Philippians 3:9, 2 Corinthians 5:11a, 2 Peter 3:9*)
Have you accepted the personal invitation from Jesus? If you have, have you been doing the job He has given you—telling people about God's invitation to them?

12 Lesson Twelve

The Wedding Guests

Theme: Tell others about Jesus.

 ## Scripture

Matthew 22:1–14

1 And Jesus answered and spake unto them again by parables, and said,

2 The kingdom of heaven is like unto a certain king, which made a marriage for his son,

3 And sent forth his servants to call them that were bidden to the wedding: and they would not come.

4 Again, he sent forth other servants, saying, Tell them which are bidden, Behold, I have prepared my dinner: my oxen and my fatlings are killed, and all things are ready: come unto the marriage.

5 But they made light of it, and went their ways, one to his farm, another to his merchandise:

6 And the remnant took his servants, and entreated them spitefully, and slew them.

7 But when the king heard thereof, he was wroth: and he sent forth his armies, and destroyed those murderers, and burned up their city.

8 Then saith he to his servants, The wedding is ready, but they which were bidden were not worthy.

9 Go ye therefore into the highways, and as many as ye shall find, bid to the marriage.

10 So those servants went out into the highways, and gathered together all as many as they found, both bad and good: and the wedding was furnished with guests.

11 And when the king came in to see the guests, he saw there a man which had not on a wedding garment:

12 And he saith unto him, Friend, how camest thou in hither not having a wedding garment? And he was speechless.

Memory Verse

Matthew 28:19
"Go ye therefore, and teach all nations, baptizing them in the name of the Father, and of the Son, and of the Holy Ghost:"

13 *Then said the king to the servants, Bind him hand and foot, and take him away, and cast him into outer darkness, there shall be weeping and gnashing of teeth.*

14 *For many are called, but few are chosen.*

Snack Suggestion

Wedding Cake
Prepare or purchase a white cake. As the children eat their "wedding" cake, give them ideas to help them tell others about Jesus.

Teacher's Checklist

- ❑ Read Matthew 22:1–14 daily.
- ❑ Study Lesson 12.
- ❑ Flash cards 12.1–12.3
- ❑ Gather for lesson—royal list of names.
- ❑ Prepare snack—white cake.
- ❑ Print "Pin the Points" game from the Ministry Resource CD.
- ❑ Print memory verse flash cards from the Ministry Resource CD.
- ❑ Gather for object lesson—simple wedding invitations, party hats, party favors.
- ❑ Gather for craft—white paper, blue cardstock, ribbon, glue, scissors.
- ❑ Print wedding invitation template for each student from the Ministry Resource CD.
- ❑ Print and duplicate Coloring Pages or Activity Pages on the Ministry Resource CD (one per student).
- ❑ Print and duplicate Take-Home Paper on the Ministry Resource CD (one per student).

The Stories of Our Saviour | © 2011 Striving Together Publications

Bible Lesson

Scripture: Matthew 22:1–14

INTRODUCING THE STORY

What is the most exciting invitation you have ever received? Sometimes we receive an invitation to a birthday party, and we get busy, planning and preparing for the party. We mark the date on the calendar. We go out and buy a gift. We take the gift home and wrap it. Then, we wait for the day of the party to come. Often, it seems like a very long time until the day finally arrives.

Sometimes we receive an invitation to a wedding. We put the invitation up on the refrigerator to remind us of the important date. We find out what the bride and groom need for their new home, so we can get them the perfect wedding gift. We find the prettiest paper or gift bag we can to wrap their gift, and we buy a card to go with it. When the day of the wedding finally arrives, we put on our best clothes, and we go to the wedding.

Jesus told a story of a wedding invitation being delivered in an unusual way. Rather than the invitations being sent in the mail, they were delivered personally by servants. Let's find out if the people were as excited to receive a wedding invitation as we are.

Teaching Tip

Allow time for discussion as students recall invitations that made them excited.
A student might say, "When someone told me Jesus wanted me in Heaven." If so, agree wholeheartedly that that is the best invitation we will ever receive. Then, you can refer to that student's response when you apply the lesson.

THE STORY

1. The First Group of Invitations Given and Refused (v. 3)

Excitement filled the castle. All the king's servants lined up before the king to receive his orders.

"As you all know, my son, the prince, is going to be married in just a few days," the king said grandly to his servants. "Here is a list for each of you. You are to go to the home of each person on your list and invite them to the wedding. It's going to be a fabulous wedding. Why, it's going to be a wedding fit for a king—or a prince!"

"The prince is going to be married, and you are invited," one servant said to the first man on his list.

"I'm not interested," the man replied. "I have too much to do. I don't have time for a wedding."

Act It Out

Royal List
Prepare a royal looking list of names and addresses, hand written or in a script-type font. Act out the part of the servants, appearing to be following your list. Go to one student after another, as the servants went to invited guests, requesting them to come to the wedding.

Flash Card 12.1

"Why wouldn't someone want to come to the royal wedding?" the servant wondered as he hurried on to the next person on his list.

He knocked on the next door. "Sir, the prince is going to be married, and you are invited to the wedding," he told the man excitedly.

"Who does the king think he is?" asked the man. "He thinks I can just drop whatever I'm doing to go to his son's wedding. Well, the king is mistaken. I, for one, won't be able to make it to the prince's wedding."

The servant went to one home after another, visiting all the people on the list the king had given him. Everyone on his list refused to come to the prince's wedding. "How could anyone refuse an invitation to the prince's wedding?" the servant asked himself. The king would be so angry. How could the servant tell him that no one on his list was coming to the wedding?

On the way back to the palace, the servant met the rest of the king's servants who had been given lists of people to invite to the prince's wedding. "You're not going to believe this, but no one on my list is going to come to the wedding," he said to the other servants. "Who would refuse an invitation to the wedding of the prince?"

"Same with my list," said a fellow servant. "Mine, too," said another. In fact, no one in the whole kingdom was coming to the prince's wedding.

2. The Second Group of Invitations Given and Refused (vv. 4–5)

When the king heard the sad news, he was patient and kind. He wondered why the people wouldn't come, and he decided to give them another chance. He called more of his servants. "Tell the people on your list," he said, "the king has the dinner all prepared. The choicest ox has been killed in honor of my son's wedding. You will feast on the finest meal that has ever been served in all the kingdom. Come now to the prince's wedding. You have a special invitation to the prince's wedding."

The first servant went to the first person on his list. He met the man returning from a hard day's work out in his field. The servant said, "The prince is going to be married today, and you have a special invitation. The dinner is all prepared—the finest meal ever to be served in all the kingdom. Come now to the prince's wedding."

"Well, isn't that sweet," laughed the man. "The prince's wedding. I hope everyone has a nice time without me, because I'm not going. I have a farm to take care of. I don't have time for the prince's wedding."

"Oh no," thought the servant, as he rushed on to the next person on his list. "I wouldn't have thought anyone would refuse an invitation to the royal wedding. The king is offering all the wonderful foods of his kingdom, and the guest has refused."

When the man answered the next door, the servant said, "The prince is getting married today. The king has prepared the finest meal ever to be served in all the kingdom, and you're invited—a special invitation from the king! Come now to the prince's wedding."

"Ha, the prince's wedding!" scoffed the man. "Well, you just tell the king that I'm not interested in any wedding for the prince. I have a job to do, money to earn. Let the king find someone who cares about the prince! Let him ask them."

3. The Servants Beaten and Killed (v. 6)

The servant continued on his journey, amazed that the guests were refusing to come to the prince's wedding. When he asked the next person on his list, the man caught the servant, beat him, and killed the king's servant!

It was the same with all the king's servants sent out that day. Each one was caught, beaten, and killed.

4. The King's Armies Commissioned (v. 7)

When the king heard the dreadful news, he was filled with anger. "They have rejected my invitation, and they have killed my servants." He called his armies. "Destroy those murderers," he commanded. And the king's armies did as they were commanded. They destroyed all those who had refused his invitation and beaten and killed his servants.

5. Everyone Given a Wedding Invitation (vv. 8–10)

There was still to be a wedding for the prince, but there were no guests. So, the king called more of his servants. "The wedding is ready, but they which were bidden were not worthy," (Matthew 22:8). "Now, go throughout the entire kingdom, inviting whomever you find. Go into the highways—go everywhere you can think of, and invite everyone. Tell them it's time for the prince's wedding.

Say, 'The king wants you to come to his son's wedding, and it's going to begin immediately!'"

This time, the king didn't give his servants a list of special people to invite. He just said, "Go to the good people, go to the bad. Invite them all! Invite everyone you meet to the prince's wedding."

6. The Wedding Filled with Guests (v. 10)

Flash Card 12.2

The servants did as they were commanded. They "went out into the highways, and gathered together all as many as they found, both bad and good: and the wedding was furnished with guests" (Matthew 22:10).

A servant walked up to a man who was weeding his garden. "Hey, the prince is getting married, and you're invited. Come on!" The man held his hat on his head as he ran along behind the servant on his way to the wedding.

"The prince is getting married today, and you're invited," said another servant to a woman who was taking care of her baby. "Hurry, or you'll be late!" The woman picked up her baby and quickly followed the servant to the wedding!

A third servant came upon a man who had just gotten out of prison. "The prince is getting married, and you're invited. Hurry up!" he called.

"Are you sure the king wants me?" the ex-prisoner asked.

"Sure—the only requirement the king has is that you wear the wedding garment you are given at the door. There's one for everybody. Now, come on!"

Finally, the wedding was filled with guests. This time, the people who were invited came to the wedding of the prince. These guests felt unworthy to be invited to such an important event—the royal wedding! And they did exactly as the servant had commanded them. When they arrived at the palace, they gladly took the robe the king had provided for each wedding guest to wear. They put on the wedding garment and took their place at the table for the wedding banquet.

7. The Guest Without a Wedding Garment (vv. 11–14)

The excited crowd was silenced as the king entered the royal banquet hall. The king was pleased as he looked about and saw the guests, all wearing the wedding garments he had provided for them. "Yes, they have come as I requested—each guest wearing the robe I have provided. No one is allowed in to the wedding wearing only his own clothes."

Suddenly, the king froze. "He saw there a man which had not on a wedding garment" (Matthew 22:11). The king said to the man, "Friend, how did you come into the feast without a wedding garment?"

Flash Card 12.3

The man didn't know what to say to the king. After all, the king had said no one could enter the royal wedding banquet without a wedding garment. The king had even provided the garment for each guest, but he had refused to put it on. There he was, wearing only his own clothes, and now the king was asking him why. He had nothing to answer the king.

"Servant," called the king, "tie this man up, take him away, and cast him into the darkness. He refused my wedding garment."

APPLYING THE STORY

This story is often called the parable of The Marriage Feast, and it's not hard to see what Jesus wanted us to learn from it.

The king in the story is God the Father, and He invites all of us to Heaven. The only way we can go to Heaven is by being clothed in the clothing that He puts on us—the clothing of righteousness. Just as the guests at the wedding feast had to be covered in the king's clothing, we need to be covered in a robe of righteousness, put on us by God when we trust Jesus as our Saviour. Now, we know that righteousness isn't really clothing, but God gives us this picture in our minds to help us understand. When we trust Jesus, God sees us as if we are covered in a robe of righteousness, because our sin is covered by Jesus' righteousness.

The way a person puts on the clothing of righteousness is by trusting Jesus Christ as his Saviour from sin. Then, instead of seeing our own sinful selves, God sees us covered in the clothing He put on us—the clothing of righteousness.

Teacher's Note

Righteousness:
"rightness; conformity to God's divine law, the perfect standard of truth and justice; holiness"

Philippians 3:9

9   *And be found in him, not having mine own righteousness, which is of the law, but that which is through the faith of Christ, the righteousness which is of God by faith.*

And, sadly, those who don't let God put His garment of righteousness on them by trusting Jesus as their Saviour will, like the guest at the wedding, be cast into outer darkness. They will go to the Lake of Fire for ever and ever.

2 Corinthians 5:11a
11a Knowing therefore the terror of the Lord, we persuade men;

Teaching Tip

Ask your students for suggestions as to who these characters might be, and what they think God wants us to learn from them.

There are some other very important characters in the parable of The Marriage Feast, and God wants us to learn from these characters in particular. (Teacher, ask for suggestions as to who these characters might be.) These important characters are the servants, and the servants are you and me.

Just as the king sent out his servants to invite guests to the wedding, our King, God, sends us out to invite others to Heaven. You see, God the Father desires that everyone receive an invitation to trust Him as their Saviour.

2 Peter 3:9
9 The Lord is…not willing that any should perish, but that all should come to repentance.

He doesn't send us out like the first group or the second group of servants—with lists of who to invite. God sends us out like the third group of servants. We have no particular people to invite—God has told us to invite everyone.

The third group of servants did exactly as the king had told them, and the wedding was filled with guests. Will Heaven be filled with people you have invited? Will there be people in Heaven who are there because you have told them that God wants everyone to go to Heaven and that He has provided the way for them to go there?

We have an exciting job to do—telling people about God's invitation to them. Just think, when we share with someone what God has done for us, and that it's for them too, we are giving them the most important invitation they will ever receive!

When the people with whom we share the invitation trust Jesus as their Saviour, we have a part in their spending forever and ever in Heaven. We will have joy in our hearts, knowing we are God's servants. What a wonderful privilege we have to be God's servants, giving out invitations from our Heavenly Father.

Since God has commanded you to give out His invitation, ask Him to show you ways to do it. Here are a few ways to get you started. God is just waiting to show you many more ways, if you'll just ask Him.

- Give a tract to someone at school, in the store, or at a park.
- Call your grandma or grandpa (or another family member—maybe an aunt, uncle, or cousin) and tell them that God wants them to go to Heaven by trusting Jesus as their Saviour.
- Tell a friend at school about your salvation. Ask them if you can share with them how to go to Heaven too.

If you know Jesus Christ as your Saviour, then you have the wonderful responsibility and opportunity to be His servant. You can help deliver the invitation to Heaven.

Sometimes people will reject the invitation you share with them, just as some rejected the king's invitation in the story. Sometimes they will tell you they are too busy or that they don't believe you. Sometimes they will just say, "No." Sometimes they will make fun of you. Sometimes they will laugh at you.

If you have given the invitation, then you have served your Heavenly Father. You have done what He commanded you to do, and you have pleased Him, whether your invitation is accepted or rejected.

If you don't know Christ as your Saviour, the invitation has been given to you—all you have to do is go to the Lord Jesus Christ and trust Him as your Saviour. Then, you will be clothed in his robe of righteousness.

Can you believe the King of kings would invite us to be clothed in His righteousness? And that He would give us the job of taking that same invitation to others?

Review Game/Questions

Pin the Points on the Map

Instructions

Print game map on 11 x 17 paper. Laminate for durability.

To Play

Divide the class into two teams. When a student answers a review question correctly, he may come to the front. Put a blind fold on and spin the student around. Give him a small sticker to place on the map. Wherever the sticker is placed the team gets that amount of points.

1. What time of celebration was the king planning?
   Answer: He was planning for a wedding for his son.

2. What did he send his servants to do?
   Answer: The servants were sent to invite guests to the wedding.

3. Did the first group of guests accept the invitation to the wedding?
   Answer: No, they did not accept the invitation.

4. Did the second group of guests accept the wedding invitations?
   Answer: No, they refused to go, as well.

5. What happened to the servants after they invited the guests?
   Answer: They were beaten and killed.

6. Who was finally invited to the wedding?
   Answer: Everyone!

7. What was the only requirement for attending the wedding?
   Answer: The guests had to wear the wedding garment provided by the king.

8. What happened to the man who refused to wear the garment?
   Answer: He was cast into darkness.

9. What does the wedding garment in our story represent?
   Answer: The wedding garment represents the clothing of righteousness given to us by God when we are saved.

10. Name some ideas for sharing God's invitation to Heaven with others.

    Answer: Answers will vary, but may include examples given on page 179.

 ## Teaching the Memory Verse

Matthew 28:19

19 Go ye therefore, and teach all nations, baptizing them in the name of the Father, and of the Son, and of the Holy Ghost:

Print flash cards from the Ministry Resource CD, and laminate for durability. Have the class open their Bibles to Matthew 28:19, and read the verse together. Remind the students that God wants us to tell everyone about Jesus!

Everyone:

Everyone wearing (call out a color), stand and recite the verse.

Everyone who has (call out a color of eyes), stand and recite the verse.

Everyone who has (call out a color of hair), stand and recite the verse.

Everyone with the letter (call out a letter) in their name, stand and recite the verse.

Everyone who's birthday is in (call out a month), stand and recite the verse.

Everyone with a Bible, stand and recite the verse.

Everyone who loves God, stand and recite the verse.

Object Lesson—You're Invited!

Materials Needed:
- Simple wedding invitations
- Party hats
- Party favors

For the Teacher:

1. Create or purchase a simple wedding or party invitation for each child and worker.

2. Distribute the invitation along with a party hat at the beginning of class (or as students arrive). You will give a party hat to workers, as well. Purposely, however, do not give a hat to one worker.

3. Tell the students that the party hat is to be worn when the celebration begins after the lesson.

To the class:

When the lesson and invitation are finished, let the class know that the party is about to begin. Walk around the room, making sure that each person attending the celebration is wearing a hat. When you come to the worker who is not wearing a hat, ask the worker where the hat is. The worker should reply that he or she does not have a hat. Then, give the worker a hat, so that everyone can participate in the party.

Application

Explain to the children that everyone was invited to the party, but not everyone came to the party with the hat, as instructed. The same is true with the invitation to Heaven. Everyone on the earth is invited to go to Heaven, but, just as the children accepted the hat, everyone who wants to go to Heaven must accept the free gift of salvation!

Craft—Sweetheart List

Getting It Together

White paper
Blue cardstock
Ribbon
Glue
Scissors

Per student:
Wedding invitation template from the Ministry Resource CD

Putting It Together

1. Print and cut out the wedding invitation template from the Ministry Resource CD.
2. Cut the blue cardstock into 7 inch by 4 inch strips.
3. Glue the wedding invitation to the cardstock.
4. Decorate the wedding invitation.

Seeing It Together

Students can us their wedding invitations as a prospect list to keep track of the people they are praying will come to church or be saved.

 # Additional Resources

Find the following items on the Ministry Resource CD:

- Coloring Page (for younger children)
- Activity Page (for older children)
- Student Take-Home Paper
- PowerPoint Presentation

Suggested Classroom Schedule

Before Class	Complete attendance record. Provide students with coloring/activity pages.
Opening	Welcome
Prayer	Prayer requests and praise reports from the children
Song Time	
Memory Verse	Romans 14:12
Song Time	
Object Lesson	Using Our Talents
Bible Lesson	The Three Men Given Talents
Application/Invitation	Help saved students apply lesson. Invite unsaved students to receive Christ.
Snack	Coin Crackers and Cheese
Review Game/ Questions	Baseball
Craft	Talents
Closing	Give announcements and pray. Distribute take-home papers.

Lesson Thirteen Overview

The Three Men Given Talents

Theme—Use your talents for God.

Scripture

Matthew 25:14–30

Memory Verse

Romans 14:12—"So then every one of us shall give account of himself to God."

Lesson Outline

Introducing the Story

Today we will learn about a story of a master trusting his servants with money. Jesus tells us this story to illustrate how He has entrusted each of us.

Telling the Story

1. **The Master Goes on a Journey** (v. 14)—*Flash Card 13.1*

2. **The Master Entrusts His Servants with His Money** (v.14)

3. **Each Servant Is Given Money** (v. 15)

4. **The Servants' Investments** (vv.16–18)—*Flash Card 13.2*

5. **Return of the Master** (v. 19, Romans 14:12)

6. **Rewards for the Servants** (vv. 20–30)—*Flash Card 13.3*

Applying the Story (1 Corinthians 4:2, 2 Corinthians 9:7, Psalm 104:33, Romans 12:13, Proverbs 4:7, John 15:8a, Ephesians 6:10, 2 Corinthians 8:12)

God has given every Christian gifts, abilities, and talents. Are you using what God has given you for His glory?

13 Lesson Thirteen

The Three Men Given Talents

Theme: Use your talents for God.

Scripture

Matthew 25:14–30

14 For the kingdom of heaven is as a man travelling into a far country, who called his own servants, and delivered unto them his goods.

15 And unto one he gave five talents, to another two, and to another one; to every man according to his several ability; and straightway took his journey.

16 Then he that had received the five talents went and traded with the same, and made them other five talents.

17 And likewise he that had received two, he also gained other two.

18 But he that had received one went and digged in the earth, and hid his lord's money.

19 After a long time the lord of those servants cometh, and reckoneth with them.

20 And so he that had received five talents came and brought other five talents, saying, Lord, thou deliveredst unto me five talents: behold, I have gained beside them five talents more.

21 His lord said unto him, Well done, thou good and faithful servant: thou hast been faithful over a few things, I will make thee ruler over many things: enter thou into the joy of thy lord.

22 He also that had received two talents came and said, Lord, thou deliveredst unto me two talents: behold, I have gained two other talents beside them.

23 His lord said unto him, Well done, good and faithful servant; thou hast been faithful over a few things, I will make thee ruler over many things: enter thou into the joy of thy lord.

24 Then he which had received the one talent came and said, Lord, I knew thee that thou art an hard man, reaping where thou hast not sown, and gathering where thou hast not strawed:

25 *And I was afraid, and went and hid thy talent in the earth: lo, there thou hast that is thine.*

26 *His lord answered and said unto him, Thou wicked and slothful servant, thou knewest that I reap where I sowed not, and gather where I have not strawed:*

27 *Thou oughtest therefore to have put my money to the exchangers, and then at my coming I should have received mine own with usury.*

28 *Take therefore the talent from him, and give it unto him which hath ten talents.*

29 *For unto every one that hath shall be given, and he shall have abundance: but from him that hath not shall be taken away even that which he hath.*

30 *And cast ye the unprofitable servant into outer darkness: there shall be weeping and gnashing of teeth.*

Teacher's Checklist

- ❑ Read Matthew 25:14–30 daily.
- ❑ Study Lesson 13.
- ❑ Flash cards 13.1–13.3
- ❑ Prepare for lesson—"Help Wanted" advertisements.
- ❑ Prepare snack—round crackers and cheese.
- ❑ Print Baseball game from the Ministry Resource CD.
- ❑ Print memory verse flash cards from the Ministry Resource CD.
- ❑ Gather for object lesson—frisbee.
- ❑ Purchase for craft—Coflex bandages, two magnets per student, one clothespin per student.
- ❑ Print—verse template and craft template for craft from the Ministry Resource CD.
- ❑ Gather for craft—crayons, scissors, glue.
- ❑ Print and duplicate Coloring Pages or Activity Pages on the Ministry Resource CD (one per student).
- ❑ Print and duplicate Take-Home Paper on the Ministry Resource CD (one per student).

Snack Suggestion

Coin Crackers and Cheese

Using a round cookie cutter, cut slices of cheese into small round shapes. Place the round pieces of cheese on round crackers. As the children enjoy their crackers and cheese, remind them to use what God has given them to bring glory to God.

 **Bible Lesson**

Scripture: Matthew 25:14–30

INTRODUCING THE STORY

Pretend you are a grown-up, and you are a millionaire! You want to hire someone to take care of your money. You would like the person you hire to take your money and use it to make more money for you.

You are preparing an advertisement for the newspaper in order to find just the right person to hire for the job. What would your ad say? (Allow time for students to answer.)

Which of the following advertisements would describe the type of person you would like to hire?

HELP WANTED

Business manager—Hard-working and skilled individual, with extensive experience, needed to oversee investments for prosperous business. This person must be creative and work well with people. Must also be willing to research opportunities and must have expert decision-making skills. Must do your best at every job you are given.

HELP WANTED

Business manager—Lazy individual, no experience needed. It is not necessary that this person be wise or know how to work with people. Must do things the same way you've always done them. No need to study or spend much time making decisions. No creativity needed for this job.

Now, which advertisement do you think Jesus would use if He were going to choose someone to work for Him? He told His disciples a story that describes exactly what Jesus is looking for in a worker.

 **Teaching Tip**

Print out these HELP WANTED advertisements on large sheets of paper or poster board, and hold up the posters for the students to read as you discuss the ads.

THE STORY

1. A Master Goes on a Journey (v. 14)

Long ago, there was a young man. This young man worked hard at every job he was given. When his mother asked him to help wash the dishes, he made sure every dish was washed, dried, and put away. Not only did he wash the dishes, but he also cleaned off the table and counter, and he swept the crumbs off the floor.

When the young man's father asked him to mow the lawn, the young man made sure he didn't miss one area of the yard. He took scissors and trimmed around each tree and bush, and he put the tools away when he was finished with his work.

When his teacher sent him on an errand, the young man immediately followed his teacher's instructions. He didn't stop and talk to people along the way, but rather, he did exactly what he was asked and gave his teacher a report when he returned.

When he was given an assignment in school, the young man didn't say to himself, "This is too hard! I don't know the answer. I can't do this." Instead, the young man listened carefully to his teacher's directions. If he didn't understand the assignment, he respectfully asked the teacher to explain it to him. Then, the young man set off to learn all he could about the subject of his assignment. If he didn't know the answers to the teacher's questions, the young man looked up the answers in books or asked other people who were experts in the subject for answers so he could finish his assignment properly and on time.

When the young man was given jobs for pay, he was very careful with the money he earned. He put some of his money into savings, and some of his money, he invested. Soon, the young man was grown, and he had earned a great deal of money. The young man became a full-grown man, and he had also become very rich.

The man bought property and hired servants to care for his property. The time came when the man needed to take a long journey to a country very far from his own. He couldn't leave his money and property without someone to care for them. The man thought about what he should do. "I want to be able to earn more money, even while I am out of the country. I know what I will do—I will give my money to my servants and give them the job of taking care of it and using it to earn more money for me while I am gone. Yes, my servants will invest my money and earn more for me while I am away!"

2. The Master Entrusts His Servants with His Money (v. 14)

The man was greatly pleased with his idea. He immediately called his three servants. When the servants stood before him, he handed them each some of his own money and instructed them to take care of it while he was gone.

Teacher's Note

Invest:
"to lay out possessions (money, property, etc.) with the expectation of gaining profit"

Flash Card 13.1

3. Each Servant Is Given Money (v. 15)

The master knew that each of his servants was different from the others, and he gave them money according to the ability each of his servants had.

The first servant had great wisdom in taking care of money, just like the master. "I know this servant will be diligent with my money. I know he will carefully invest it to earn more money to give me at my return," the master thought. To this first servant, the kind master gave five talents—an enormous amount of money—to care for. "Use this money wisely while I am away," the master instructed him.

The second servant wasn't yet as experienced as the first servant. He was younger, and he hadn't earned as much money, and he hadn't invested as much money, as the first servant. But he had often made wise decisions with his money. "This young man will be careful and do his best with the money I give him," the master thought. The kind master gave this second servant two talents—less than the first servant, but a very large sum of money, just the same. "Use this money wisely," the good master said to his second servant.

"My third servant has the ability to invest my money wisely," the master said to himself. "But he is not always diligent, and he takes a lot of breaks when he ought to be working. I will give him one talent, and we will see what he does with it." The kind master gave his third servant one talent, which was not as much as he gave the first two servants, but, still a large amount of money. "Use this money wisely," the master instructed the third servant.

Teacher's Note

A "talent" is a weight of a particular substance—generally a precious metal. The value of a talent, therefore, would vary, depending upon the substance being weighed. A talent of silver would be the equivalent of 6,000 denarii—that is, 6,000 days' hire for the average working man. A talent of silver would work out roughly to $200,000 by today's standards, and a talent of gold would have a much higher value.

4. The Servants' Investments (vv. 16–18)

The first servant couldn't believe how much money his master had given him. "I have such a good master," he thought. "He has entrusted me with a great sum of money, and I will do my best to use it wisely to earn more money for him. He has taught me so much. He has always taken what he has and done his very best with it, and I would like to be just like him. I will try to do with his money exactly what he would do if he were here."

The first servant worked diligently, investing his five talents. After some time, he had earned five more talents for his master. "The master so kindly gave me five talents before he left," the servant said happily to himself, "and I have been able to double the master's money. Now I have ten talents to

Flash Card 13.2

give to my master when he returns." And the servant rejoiced as he thought of how happy his master would be when he returned.

The second servant looked at the two talents the master had left in his care. "My master is so generous to me," he thought. "I don't deserve his generosity or his trust. He has worked so hard to earn his money, and now he is giving me the opportunity to use it to earn more. I'm going to do my very best to earn as much money as I can for him. I am going to try to do just what the master would do with this money, if he were here."

The second servant worked diligently, investing his two talents. His hard work paid off, and before his master returned, he earned two more talents to give to his master on his return from the far country. "I can't believe I will have four whole talents to give to my master when he returns," the servant said to himself. "I'm so thankful my master trusted me, and I am so happy he will be proud of me."

The third servant looked at his one talent and thought, "Ha! Imagine that—my master only gave me one talent, when my fellow servants got so much more. I deserve better than this! Why should I make more money for my master, anyway? He already has so much—why does he need more? I have other things to do with my time than to make money for someone who already has so much. I need more sleep, for instance. And I need to have some time just to relax and enjoy myself. I need time for fun. I need to take care of me—not some old master!"

"Let's see…I can't spend my talent on myself, or my master will be very angry with me. I can't give it to my friends. If I keep it in my house until the master returns, someone might find out that I have it and try to steal it. I know what I'll do—I'll bury it in the ground, where it will be safe until my master comes home. Then, when he returns, I'll give him his talent back, safe and sound. He gave me one talent, and he shall have one talent when he comes home." So, the unfaithful servant who wasn't interested in serving his master took his one talent and buried it in the ground.

5. Return of the Master (v. 19)

The master's business in the far country was finished, and it was time for him to return home. He had wondered, while he was away in the far country, how his three servants had done with their investments.

Romans 14:12

12   So then every one of us shall give account of himself to God.

6. Rewards for the Servants (vv. 20–30)

This was the day the first two servants—the faithful servants—had long awaited. They couldn't wait to see their master's pleasure when they showed him what they had done with their talents.

The master called for the first servant—the one who had been given five talents. "What have you done with the five talents I gave you?" the master asked.

"And so he that had received five talents came and brought other five talents, saying, Lord, thou deliveredst unto me five talents: behold, I have gained beside them five talents more" (Matthew 25:20).

The master said to the first servant, "Well done, thou good and faithful servant: thou hast been faithful over a few things, I will make thee ruler over many things: enter thou into the joy of thy lord" (Matthew 25:21). The first servant was happy about the praise his master gave him. He was happy that his master was rewarding him by giving him much more to take care of for his master. But he was especially happy that he had been able to help his master, who had been so good to him. He was thrilled to give his master joy.

Then the master called the second servant, who had been given two talents. "Before I left on my journey, I gave you two talents. What have you done with them?"

"He also that had received two talents came and said, Lord, thou deliveredst unto me two talents: behold, I have gained two other talents beside them" (Matthew 25:22).

The master said to the second servant, "Well done, good and faithful servant; thou hast been faithful over a few things, I will make thee ruler over many things: enter thou into the joy of thy lord" (Matthew 25:23). Like the first servant, the second servant was excited about the reward and praise he had been given, but he was more pleased that he had served and helped his master. And he was thrilled to have brought joy to his master.

Then the master called in the third servant—the one who had received one talent. He wondered whether or not the servant had wisely used his money. He said to his servant, "And what have you done with the money I gave you?"

Teacher's Note

Interest:
"The fee charged by a lender to a borrower for the use of borrowed money"

Flash Card 13.3

"Well sir," the servant said, "I knew that you are a hard man. You harvest where you haven't planted, and you take in money that you didn't have to work hard for. Nothing ever pleases you. I knew you were like that. And I was afraid, and went and hid thy talent in the earth: lo, there thou hast that is thine" (Matthew 25:25).

The third servant wasn't expecting what happened next. Instead of praising the third servant, the master said to him, "You have been a wicked and lazy servant. You knew me. You knew that I use the money I have to earn more money. You knew that I harvest where I haven't planted. You should have at least taken my money and put it in the bank. Then, when I returned home, I would have had the one talent I gave you, plus interest."

The master commanded, "Take the one talent from this man and give it to the man with ten talents. I know I can trust him to wisely use it and increase it. Take this unprofitable servant away!"

APPLYING THE STORY

Whom do you think the master—the one who gave talents to his servants to use for him—in this story represents? (Allow time for students to answer.) God is the Master in this story, and He is the Giver of all we—His servants—have. He gives us salvation. He gives us our families. He gives us our houses, clothing, and food. He gives us our games and tools. He gives us our talents and abilities. Everything we have comes from our good God.

God gives us each what He wants us to have. He gives some people a lot of money, He gives some people a little money, and He gives some people a medium amount of money. He gives some people big, fancy houses, and He gives some people small apartments. He gives some people the ability to sing beautifully, and to some people, He doesn't give the ability to sing. He gives some people the ability to play a musical instrument, and to some people He doesn't give that ability. He gives some people great skill in school work (academics), and to some people He doesn't give that skill. He gives some people an extremely outgoing personality, and He gives some people a quiet personality. He gives some people the know-how to fix mechanical things, and to some people He doesn't give that know-how. He gives some people the ability to figure out mathematical problems, He gives some people the ability to write poetry, and He gives some people an understanding of science, history, or language.

But our Master, the Lord, gives everybody something! And, like the master in the story, God wants us to use what He gives us for Him. He wants us to remember that all we have actually belongs to Him.

Do you remember what the two faithful servants wanted to do with their master's money? They wanted to use it exactly as the master would have used it if he had been there.

That is God's plan for His servants, as well. He wants us to use what He gives us just as He would use it if He were here.

1 Corinthians 4:2

2   *Moreover it is required in stewards, that a man be found faithful.*

When He gives you money, He wants you to tithe first of all, and then use the rest in the way He would use it. What would Jesus spend His money on? Would He give to others? He wants to show you through His Word, the Bible. He also wants you to ask Him.

2 Corinthians 9:7

7   *Every man according as he purposeth in his heart, so let him give; not grudgingly, or of necessity: for God loveth a cheerful giver.*

If He gives you a good singing voice, He wants you to use it for Him. He may want you to sing in a choir or a singing group at church. He wants you to use your singing voice to sing songs about Jesus to your little sister or brother. He wants you to sing happily as you clean your room. He wants you to use your voice to sing hymns to an elderly person in a nursing home. He wants to show you through His Word, the Bible, how to use your voice for Him. He also wants you to ask Him.

Psalm 104:33

33   *I will sing unto the LORD as long as I live: I will sing praise to my God while I have my being.*

Do you have a beautiful house? How would God want you to use your house? Do you ask your parents if you can invite someone over to your

Teaching Tip

Teacher, add gifts and abilities that you know various students in your class possess, desire, or lack. Ask the Lord to show you examples that will "hit home" with your students.

house who doesn't have many friends—someone who would feel loved if you shared your home with him or her? He wants to show you through His Word, the Bible, how to use your house for Him. He also wants you to ask Him.

Romans 12:13

13 Distributing to the necessity of saints; given to hospitality.

Do you have the ability to get good grades in school? Do you do your best to learn all you can so you can use your mental abilities to your fullest potential for the Lord? Do you seek God's wisdom and understanding? Do you graciously help others who may not have the same academic gift that you have? (Of course, you would never give someone answers to an assignment or test—you would only explain something to them that they don't understand!) God wants to show you through His Word, the Bible, how He wants you to use your mind for Him. He also wants you to ask Him.

Proverbs 4:7

7 Wisdom is the principal thing; therefore get wisdom: and with all thy getting get understanding.

Do you have an outgoing personality? Do you use it to welcome visitors to Sunday school and church? Do you share with others how they can know Jesus as their Saviour? God wants to show you through His Word, the Bible, how to use your personality for Him, and He also wants you to ask Him.

John 15:8a

8a Herein is my Father glorified, that ye bear much fruit:

When He gives you strength, He wants you to use it for Him. He wants you to work hard, He wants you to help others, and He wants you to exercise and build strong muscles so you can be healthy to serve Him. God wants to show you through His Word, the Bible, how to use your strength for Him, and He also wants you to ask Him.

Ephesians 6:10

10 Finally, my brethren, be strong in the Lord, and in the power of his might.

Even if you don't have a beautiful singing voice, He wants you to use the voice you do have for Him. Even if you don't have a lot of money, He wants you to use the money you do have for Him. Even if you don't have a large, beautiful house, He wants you to use the house you do have for Him. Even if you are not as smart as someone else in your class, He wants you to use the mind you do have for Him. He wants you to do your best with every single thing He gives to you. He wants you to use it like He would if He were here.

2 Corinthians 8:12

12   *For if there be first a willing mind, it is accepted according to that a man hath, and not according to that he hath not.*

God has given every Christian gifts, abilities, and talents. Some people have more than others. God doesn't ask you to give Him talents that He hasn't given to you. He only wants you to take what He has given you and use it for Him. He wants you to make Him known to others through the gifts He gives you.

Do you remember what happened to the two faithful servants who took the talents their master gave them and used them to earn more for him? (Allow students to answer.) The master gave them much more to take care of for him. And, that's what God will do for you—His servant—when you use the gifts He gives you for Him.

Something else happened to the two faithful servants. Their master shared his joy with them, and God will share His joy with you when you serve Him with the gifts He gives you. God is so loving and kind to each one of us.

Teaching Tip

At end of lesson, pass out pieces of paper and have your students list talents and gifts God has given to them. (If a child struggles to write a list, help him identify potential gifts or talents.) Encourage them to write down how they can use each specific gift for Him, and end with a prayer, encouraging students to dedicate their gifts and talents to God to use for His glory.

Review Game/Questions

Baseball

Instructions

Print game pieces from the Ministry Resource CD. Cut and laminate for durability.

Divide class into two teams. Ask Team 1 a review question. If students answer correctly, they come to the front and pick a baseball. Reveal the points on the back. Then have the student pick a glove from your hand. This determines who catches the points. Award the points to the team on the glove. Repeat with Team 2. The team with the most points wins.

1. Where did the master in our story go?
   Answer: On a journey

2. How many talents did the master give to his first servant?
   Answer: Five talents

3. What did the first two servants do with the talents they were given?
   Answer: They doubled them.

4. How many talents did the third servant receive from his master?
   Answer: One talent

5. What did the third servant do with the talent he was given?
   Answer: He buried it.

6. What did the master say to the first two servants who invested wisely?
   Answer: "Well done."

7. Was the master pleased with the third servant for burying his talent?
   Answer: No.

8. Who represents the master and servants in our story?
   Answer: God is the master, and we are the servants.

9. Do we all have some talent or gift from God?
   Answer: Yes!

10. What are some ways we can use our gifts for the Lord?
    Answer: Answers will vary.

 # Teaching the Memory Verse

Romans 14:12

12 So then every one of us shall give account of himself to God.

Print and laminate flash cards. Read Romans 14:12 several times.

Say to the class, "One day each of us will stand before the Lord, and He will evaluate our works. Are we taking the talents and abilities that God has given us and using them for His glory?"

Have two to four students come to the board and have them write the verse as quickly as possible. The first one who writes the verse correctly gets a piece of candy.

If you do not have a chalk or dry erase board pass out papers to entire class and have them write the verse. The first one to finish receives a piece of candy.

Object Lesson—Using Our Talents

Materials Needed:

Frisbee

Lesson:

I have a Frisbee with me today! Now, many of you have probably seen a Frisbee before, but let's pretend for a minute that we have never seen one. If you have never seen a Frisbee, maybe you would think that it was a hat. Perhaps you would think the Frisbee was a plate or even some sort of tool to dig up sand!

We all know however, that this Frisbee serves a fun and specific purpose: it flies! The Frisbee may not look like much fun, but in reality, it is a blast to play with a Frisbee! The Frisbee may not look impressive, especially in a world full of high-tech electronic toys, but it can fly really well!

Application:

Sometimes, we look at the talents God has given to us, and we may think that God hasn't given us much. We might be tempted to covet someone else's talent or to hide our own out of embarrassment or insecurity! But, God gave you just the talent He wanted you to have. It's impressive to Him, and that's all that matters! When we use our talents for a specific purpose, just like the Frisbee is used specifically for flying, God blesses it and uses it for His glory!

Additional Resources

Find the following items on the Ministry Resource CD:

- Coloring Page (for younger children)
- Activity Page (for older children)
- Student Take-Home Paper
- PowerPoint Presentation

Craft—Talents

Getting It Together

Coflex bandages
Crayons
Scissors
Glue

Per student:

1   template from Lesson 13 craft template
1   verse template located on the Ministry Resource CD
1   clothespin
2   magnets

Putting It Together

1.   Print and cut out the verse and craft template from Lesson 13.
2.   Color each box.
3.   Glue the verse to the clothespin.
4.   Glue magnets to the back of the craft.
5.   Clip the clothespin to the side of the Sunday-Saturday chart.
6.   The students can write down a talent they can do each day for the Lord.

Seeing It Together

This week, strive to use your talent every day for the Lord!

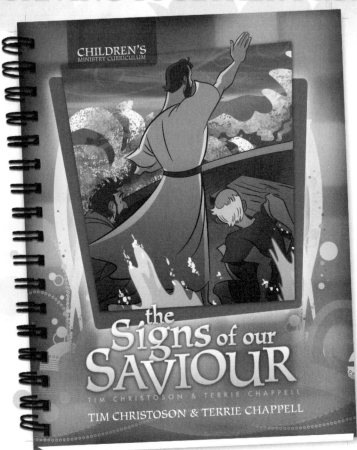